T0339857

"*Impact and the Management Researcher* is an outstanding contribution to the debate among management academics about 'what is real impact of their work, and how do we measure it'. The author, a very distinguished scholar, is leading the charge internationally to get business schools, government and funders to understand the importance of management research in terms of changing practice and policies rather than journal rankings of impact. This book is a must read by all Deans of business schools, university Presidents and funders of management research".

Sir Cary L. Cooper, *CBE, 50th Anniversary Professor of Organizational Psychology & Health, ALLIANCE Manchester Business School, University of Manchester, UK.*

"This book is a remarkable piece of scholarship. Written by a leader in the field, Usha Haley presents both original research and a concise survey of the key issues in achieving (or failing to achieve) impact in management research. Usha Haley is both a distinguished researcher and has influenced policy around the world and the skills required for this rare combination are in evidence in this book. It is critical but also offers a way forward that is practical for scholars; it is international, drawing examples from many areas of the world, and yet provides a perspective that rings true when addressing issues at a local level; and it combines insight into both qualitative and quantitative approaches with equal balance. This is a very significant book for all of us who aspire to excellence and relevance in management research".

Nic Beech, *Vice-Chancellor, Middlesex University, UK, and President of the British Academy of Management.*

"Since its establishment as an academic discipline, scholars in Management have been wracked by a core dilemma: How to gain legitimacy as a theory-grounded science while still staying relevant and having a practical impact? This book, and the ground-breaking research on which it is based, tackles this dilemma head on. Beyond being required reading for Deans and T&P Committee members, the findings presented in this book deserve careful study by all those involved in and concerned with the future of management generally, and management education and research in particular".

Peter A. Bamberger, *Domberger Chair in Organization & Management, Tel Aviv University's Coller School of Management, Israel and Research Director, Cornell University's Smithers Institute, USA.*

Impact and the Management Researcher

Universities, governments, faculty-evaluation committees, grant-bestowing institutions, scholars, and accreditation organizations have increasingly insisted on identifying and placing value on research impact. Valuation of research and scholarly output predicts innovation, affects careers, and guides resource allocations worldwide.

This book joins the burgeoning conversation in management and the social sciences with theoretical and applied discussions of the concepts, measurements, costs, and benefits that accrue to pursuing scholarly impact. The author draws on a pioneering study by the Academy of Management that asked its global membership of 20,000 how they assessed scholarly impact, including rankings and impact factors, and how institutions supported this pursuit. Through qualitative and quantitative cross-country analysis by professorial rank, geographical region, and support for various metrics, as well as exploration of parallel discussions in the social and hard sciences, the author argues for an urgent re-examination of the visible and invisible hands of research evaluation that shape lives and global societies.

This book presents original data on the external impacts of management research on policy, through the media, and in interest displayed by constituencies, which will make the book of interest to researchers, academics, and students in the fields of business and management. Recommendations from leading management scholars and from the data follow for more valid, more reliable, and less cynical metrics of research impact.

Usha C. V. Haley is W. Frank Barton Distinguished Chair in International Business, and Professor of Management, Wichita State University, USA. Her bio is at ushahaley.academia.edu.

BRITISH ACADEMY
OF MANAGEMENT

Management Impact
Series Editors: **Jean M. Bartunek, Nic Beech** *and* **Cary Cooper**

Scholarly research into business and management proliferates globally. Its impact into management practice can be difficult to monitor and measure. This series, published in association with The British Academy of Management, presents Shortform books that demonstrate how management scholarship has impacted upon the real world.

Incorporating case study examples and highlighting the link between scholarship, policy and practice, the series provides an essential resource for postgraduate students and researchers seeking to understand how to create impact through their work. The concise nature of the books also ensures that they can be useful reading for reflective practitioners.

Delivering Impact in Management Research
When Does it Really Happen?
Robert MacIntosh, Katy Mason, Nic Beech and Jean M. Bartunek

Impact and the Management Researcher
Usha C. V. Haley

For more information about this series, please visit: www.routledge.com/Management-Impact/book-series/IMPACTM

Impact and the Management Researcher

Usha C. V. Haley

Routledge
Taylor & Francis Group

LONDON AND NEW YORK

First published 2022
by Routledge
2 Park Square, Milton Park, Abingdon, Oxon OX14 4RN

and by Routledge
605 Third Avenue, New York, NY 10158

Routledge is an imprint of the Taylor & Francis Group, an informa business

© 2022 Usha C.V. Haley

The right of Usha C.V. Haley to be identified as author of this work
has been asserted in accordance with sections 77 and 78 of the
Copyright, Designs and Patents Act 1988.

All rights reserved. No part of this book may be reprinted or
reproduced or utilised in any form or by any electronic, mechanical,
or other means, now known or hereafter invented, including
photocopying and recording, or in any information storage or
retrieval system, without permission in writing from the publishers.

Trademark notice: Product or corporate names may be trademarks
or registered trademarks, and are used only for identification and
explanation without intent to infringe.

British Library Cataloguing-in-Publication Data
A catalogue record for this book is available from the British Library

Library of Congress Cataloging-in-Publication Data
Names: Haley, Usha C. V., author.
Title: Impact and the management researcher /
Usha C.V. Haley.
Description: Abingdon, Oxon ; New York, NY : Routledge, 2022. |
Series: Management impact | Includes bibliographical references
and index.
Identifiers: LCCN 2021032316 (print) | LCCN 2021032317 (ebook) |
ISBN 9780367278267 (hbk) | ISBN 9781032162959 (pbk) |
ISBN 9780429298981 (ebk)
Subjects: LCSH: Management. | Social sciences—Research.
Classification: LCC HD31.2 .H355 2022 (print) |
LCC HD31.2 (ebook) | DDC 658.0072—dc23
LC record available at https://lccn.loc.gov/2021032316
LC ebook record available at https://lccn.loc.gov/2021032317

ISBN: 978-0-367-27826-7 (hbk)
ISBN: 978-1-032-16295-9 (pbk)
ISBN: 978-0-429-29898-1 (ebk)

DOI: 10.4324/9780429298981

Typeset in Times New Roman
by codeMantra

Contents

Illustrations

Acknowledgments

This book did not arise fully formed from the author's mind. Though differing from the Academy of Management's (AOM's) report on Scholarly Impact for which I served as Product Champion, this book builds on conversations, insights, and data that the team undertook for the AOM's Strategic Initiative on Impact. Specifically, I gratefully acknowledge that teams' contributions several years ago, including from Melanie Page, Tyrone Pitsis, Kuo Frank Yu, and José Luis Rivas, some of whom authored or co-authored parts of that report that they updated for this book. Additionally, I am grateful to the AOM for providing access to the data that we collected on scholarly impact.

The AOM put its money where its mouth is by supporting the Strategic Initiative on Impact. To the best of my knowledge, the AOM remains the only major academic association that has asked its members for their views on scholarly impact – rather than just assuming them. I thank Gayle Baugh, Pamela Barr, and Peter Bamberger, sequential liaisons from the AOM's Board of Governors to the Practice Theme Committee (PTC, which I co-chaired), for their ideas, feedback, comments, advice, and help over the AOM project. Peter liberally edited (rewrote) parts of the PTC's report on plane flights from the United States to Israel – and indeed, made the report much better! I thank Lucy Leety-Wheeler, the AOM's Governance Coordinator, for her advice and help.

Finally, I thank my husband, George, for reading this manuscript, and for his general support over the years; and my daughter, Lena, for letting me work at home on sunny weekends. The views espoused in this book, and any errors, are mine alone and not of any association or institution with which I am affiliated.

Author's Bio

Usha Haley is W. Frank Barton Distinguished Chair in International Business, and Professor of Management, Wichita State University, USA. She is also Director, Center for International Business Advancement, and elected Chair, World Trade Council of Wichita. She has over 300 publications and presentations, including 8 books, and articles in venues such as the *Journal of International Business Studies, Human Relations,* the *Journal of Management Studies, Harvard Business Review,* and *California Management Review,* on non-market economies, innovation, subsidies, multinational corporations, emerging markets, trade, strategy, and scholarly impact. Usha served as co-Chair of the Academy of Management's (AOM's) Practice Theme Committee, and as Product Champion for the AOM's Report on *Measuring and Achieving Scholarly Impact.* She serves as lead editor for the *Academy of Management Learning & Education's* special issue on "Learning and Education Strategies for Scholarly Impact".

She has had regulatory influence over 40 times, with her research incorporated into federal trade regulation in the United States, EU, Australia, and India including the Non-market Economy Trade Remedy Act (the basis of HR 1229 in the USA) and three pieces of EU anti-dumping regulation. Competitive research grants include from the National Science Foundation (sole PI) on technology and innovation in energy. Her research has been covered over 500 times in the major international media including multiple times in venues such as the *Economist, Wall Street Journal, NPR's Marketplace,* and the *New York Times.* Major awards/recognitions include the *AOM's* Practice Impact Award for scholarly impact and for "Truly Outstanding Leadership and Service"; the *Economist's* "Thought

Leader" on emerging markets; Emerald Publishing's *Lifetime Achievement Award*; *American Made Hero* for supporting US manufacturing; and the Indian government sponsored *Glorious India Award* for academic contributions by diaspora to their adopted countries. For contact information, see ushahaley.academia.edu

1 Measurement matters

Usha C. V. Haley

This chapter begins with discussing some of the conversations around scholarly impact generally, and about journal rankings and the Journal Impact Figure specifically. Next, I discuss some societal costs associated with scholarly impact measures. Finally, I identify how the Academy of Management (AOM) study on scholarly impact fits into the conversation.

1.1 Conversations around scholarly impact

Over the last decade, measurements and understandings of scholarly impact in the social sciences generally, and in the Management academic discipline specifically, have become increasingly debated, discussed, and dissected. As **Figure 1.1** shows, in the AOM's and the British Academy of Management's (BAM) major academic journals, mentions of "Impact" have increased gently since 2000, and steeply since 2018. Conversations around impact have widened, led by the UK's Research Excellence Framework (REF, 2021) that increased the weight that funding agencies place on impact with elaborate measurement frameworks.

Scholarly impact measures aim to quantify and to monitor the importance of research performance. Metrics include citations or bibliometrics by article, author, publication, or institution, and various altmetrics that tabulate attention on scholarly topics, not necessarily in published articles, but on social media and other platforms. Decisions on funding, rankings of researchers, and benchmarking of institutions often depend heavily on scholarly impact measures. Peter Drucker (1974) identified some of the benefits of measuring performance and results as crucial to effectiveness: "Work implies not only that somebody is supposed to do the job, but

DOI: 10.4324/9780429298981-1

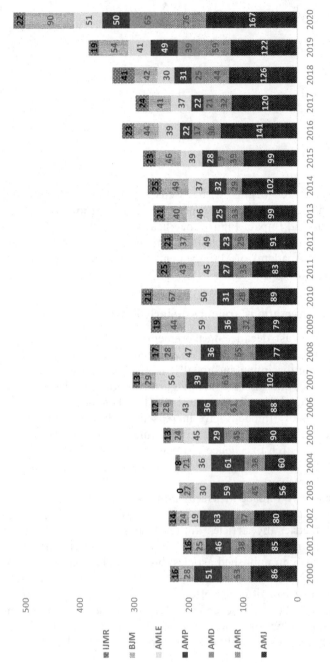

Figure 1.1 Mentions of Impact by Year in AOM and BAM Journals, 2000–2020

also accountability, a deadline and, finally, the measurement of results—that is, feedback from results on the work and on the planning process itself".

Metrics that educational institutions around the world use include journal rankings and Clarivate's Journal Impact Figures (hereafter referred to as the Impact Factor) that produce these rankings. National research performance frameworks and rankings prioritize research in high-ranked journals (Adler & Harzing, 2009). Publish or perish pressures characterize U.S. higher education; other countries are following the U.S. model, as we show later in the book, creating "international competition for legitimacy and space in a few top-tier journals" (Tsui, 2013: 175).

Few measures have exerted greater influence than the Impact Factor. Initially developed to help librarians' purchasing decisions on journals (see Garfield, 2006), the Impact Factor has transmogrified into an evaluation of the quality of individual publications and of individual researchers (Amin & Mabe, 2003; Arnold & Fowler, 2010). The measure has come under extensive scrutiny and criticism: as an inaccurate estimate of citations to any article within a specific journal (Callaway, 2016; Lariviere et al., 2016), as easy to manipulate (McVeigh & Mann, 2009; Tort et al., 2012), and with no associations to objective measures of quality (Yeung, 2017; Brembs, 2018), among other reasons. Begun over a decade ago, and as of May 2021, 19,688 individuals and organizations in 145 countries had signed the San Francisco Declaration on Research Assessment (DORA see https://sfdora.org) that critiques uses of the Impact Factor as a surrogate measure of quality for individual articles and researchers. For an excellent critique of the Impact Factor, see Lariviere and Sugimoto (2019).

Yet, a study of more than 860 review, promotion, and tenure documents from 129 universities and 381 of their academic units across Canada and the United States found that more than 40 percent of research-intensive institutions and 18 percent of master's institutions mentioned the Impact Factor (McKiernan et al. 2019). The study also identified over a dozen terms that alluded to the Impact Factor in these review, promotion, and tenure documents, without mentioning it explicitly, suggesting that the authors' methodology may have significantly underrepresented the metric's use. Of the institutions that mentioned the Impact Factor, 87 percent supported its use, with only 13 percent expressing caution; none heavily criticized the Impact Factor or prohibited its use. Similarly, researchers (O'Carroll et al., 2017) found that 68 percent of the 154 European universities they surveyed used the Impact Factor as a measure of scholarly impact.

1.2 Social costs of scholarly impact measures

Societal costs and benefits accrue to all measures of impact. Indeed "when a measure becomes a target, it ceases to be a good measure" (Strathern, 1997 on Goodhart's Law) often resulting in gaming the metrics to produce the desired measure (see Biagioli & Lippman, 2020). Measures of scholarly impact result in tradeoffs within universities on distributing spending among teaching, service, and high-level research. Christian Terwiesch and Karl Ulrich (2014) from the University of Pennsylvania's Wharton School of Business estimated that the cost of a single scholarly article authored by business-school professors amounted to US$400,000. Their report estimated a faculty's salary, benefits, and overhead per year at US$300,000; allocated time to research as 50 percent; number of A journal articles produced per year as .75; and number of authors per articles as 2. The accidental finding resulted from the authors' efforts to assess how technology could impact the costs associated with running an elite business school. One of the report's authors, Karl Ulrich, observed,

> It cost Wharton US$250,000 on our entire MOOC (Massively Open Online Course) activity last year which gets you to about page 12 on a single article...We better figure out how to articulate the value proposition. It is really important to explicitly fund scholarship and say why it is important.
>
> (quoted in Byrne, 2014)

Besides business schools, the value proposition arising from time spent on scholarship aimed at A-level journals also needs articulation for academics that spend their lives in these systems, societies that expend resources, and students that aspire for an education. The US National Science Foundation (NSF) requires all grant-funded research projects to include a discussion of "Broader Impacts", or the potential to benefit society and to contribute to achieving specific, desired societal outcomes. However, many research centers and universities face significant challenges in meeting these goals. Realities of award sizes and durations also confound unique, innovative, and assessable activities that may generate broader impacts. Consequently, mid-term and long-term effects of pursuing scholarly impact necessarily remain obfuscated at societal levels (see Adetunji & Renoe, 2017 for some efforts).

Though not dealing directly with the Impact Factor, some research indicates that scientific output approximates a curvilinear function indicating diminishing marginal returns: as funding per researcher increases, beyond a certain point, productivity decreases. Wahls (2018) reported that such diminishing marginal returns applied to U.S. National Institutes of Health (NIH) grants. Analyses of data (2006–2015) for a representative cross-section of institutions, whose funding ranged from US$3 million to US$440 million per year, revealed robust inverse correlations between funding (per institution, per award, per investigator) and scientific output (publication productivity and citation-impact productivity). Prestigious institutions had on average 65 percent higher success rates for grant applications and 50 percent larger award sizes; however, less-prestigious institutions produced 65 percent more publications and had a 35 percent higher citation-impact per dollar of funding. These findings suggest that implicit biases and social-prestige mechanisms, such as Impact Factors, powerfully influence where federal dollars go and net returns to taxpayers' investments. The findings thereby support evidence-based changes in funding policy geared towards more equitable, more diverse, and more productive measures of scholarly impact and prestige. Indeed, Willmott (2011) discussed the perversion of journal-list fetishism which devalues scholarly work that many would consider first-rate in terms of originality, significance, and rigor because it appears in lesser-ranked journals, with potentially damaging consequences for research funding.

Chavarro et al. (2017) provided data and analysis to show that the inclusion of journals in the most prestigious citation database, Clarivate's Web of Science (WoS), which also publishes Journal Citation Reports and the Impact Factor, stems from subjective criteria. Specifically, journals' countries of origin, languages, and disciplines influenced probabilities of inclusion, regardless of editorial quality or scientific impact. Consequently, Colombian journals had lower chances of being in WoS compared to Spanish journals with similar scientific impact and editorial quality. Indeed, the WoS focused on journals from the United States, and northern and western Europe; on natural sciences; and on the English language, ignoring topics of interest to many countries and stakeholders around the world.

1.3 Contributing to the conversation

To lead development of valid and reliable measures of scholarship evaluation, the AOM published an empirical report on *Measuring and Achieving Scholarly Impact* (Haley et al., 2017). With about 20,000 members worldwide, the AOM forms the preeminent scholarly association in management, publishing some of the most prestigious, high-impact, academic journals. The project had two interrelated parts: a qualitative study, and quantitative all-Academy survey on scholarly impact and its meaning to the AOM's stakeholders that included academics, managers, policymakers, and graduate students. This report included the first survey of membership from a major academic association on what constitutes scholarly impact and which stakeholders have importance for scholarly research. To date, and to the best of my knowledge, the impact study also remains the only such project undertaken by a major academic association.

For our AOM study, we began through open-ended, in-depth interviews with 30 members identified by the AOM's Board of Governors as highly impactful (e.g., journal editors, AOM Presidents, and Fellows) to identify themes; we followed this up with ten in-depth interviews of that group for analysis. The subsequent membership survey had a response rate of 19 percent. Despite their ubiquity as measures of scholarly impact, most respondents (60 percent) indicated that **journal rankings and lists**, including Impact Factors, probably did not (20 percent), definitely did not (8 percent), or might or might not (32 percent) reflect scholarly impact. A minority (about 41 percent) indicated that rankings and lists definitely reflected (7 percent) or probably reflected (34 percent) scholarly impact.

Conversely, the top five **indicators of scholarly impact** on a five-point scale (1 = very unimportant, to 5 = very important) were: Scholarly articles in top-tier journals – 4.49; Scholarly citations to research – 4.21; Scholarly books – 3.94; Competitive research grants – 3.93; and Articles in practitioner-oriented/industry publications – 3.88.

Citations have wide usage as a metric for scholarly impact; indeed, 61 percent of EU universities used citations to demonstrate scholarly impact (see O'Carroll et al., 2017, *op. cit.*). Yet, some research has shown that even in the hard sciences, citations may not correlate with individual researchers' notions on what constitutes impactful research. Researchers asked academics to look at 63 articles from one issue of the *Journal of the American Chemical Society* and to identify up to 3 articles in the issue that they thought as: the most significant (allowing the respondents to define significance); the most highly cited; the articles they would share with other chemists; and the articles they would share more broadly. Data from more than 350 respondents showed that they chose different articles for each of the four questions, though some questions correlated more highly than others. Significant and highly cited articles had the highest correlation at .9, while articles to share with chemists and articles to share broadly had the lowest correlation at .64. The researchers (Borchardt et al., 2018) concluded that respondents saw differences in impactful research: a strikingly large discrepancy existed between researchers' perceptions of impact and the metrics we currently use to measure impact. Simkin and Roychowdhury (2002) estimated the percentage of people who cited a paper that had also read it. The researchers' method drew on stochastic modeling of citations that explains empirical studies of misprint distributions in citations (which they show followed a Zipf law). They estimated that only about 20 percent of citers read the original article. Perhaps perceptions of the authors' and journals' prestige influenced citations.

Reflecting the historical focus on internal **audiences for academic research**, on a five-point scale (1 = very unimportant, to 5 = very important), respondents in our AOM study saw the top five research audiences as: Other academics in management – 4.48; Top management and decision-makers in companies – 4.26; Government and policymakers – 4.08; Other academics in the social sciences – 4.06; and Students – 4.0. Yet, about 54 percent of the survey's respondents considered **impact on practice** as either strongly important (31 percent) or intensely important (23 percent); only 7 percent viewed impact on practice as not at all important as a component of scholarly impact. Similarly, about 46 percent of survey respondents considered **impact on government policy** as either strongly important (27 percent) or intensely important (19 percent); only 10 percent viewed impact on government policy as not at all important as a component of scholarly impact.

Though more difficult to publish, about 59 percent of the respondents viewed **interdisciplinary research**, as probably more impactful (31 percent) or definitely more impactful (28 percent) than research that draws on one discipline; just 4 percent of the membership viewed interdisciplinary research as definitely not more impactful than research drawing on one discipline. Our study also revealed that Management scholars saw interdisciplinary research as more difficult to conduct and to publish in the top journals.

Supporting other studies, respondents overwhelmingly saw **institutional support** as very strong for publications in A-level journals, with other activities receiving far less, if any, support. On a five-point scale (1 = very unimportant, to 5 = very important), respondents ranked the top five beneficiaries of institutional support as: Publications in top-tier journals – 4.54; Scholarly citations to research – 3.76; Obtaining research grants – 3.64; Published books – 3.07; and Publications in practitioner journals – 2.84.

Despite prevailing rhetoric on serving society, most respondents (47 percent) saw their institutions as only sometimes supporting their

personal pursuit of scholarly impact. About 38 percent said their institution supported their pursuit almost every time (27 percent) or every
time (11 percent). About 16 percent indicated their institutions almost
never supported (13 percent) or never supported (3 percent) their pursuit of scholarly impact.

On the **influence of the field**, generally, the AOM's membership
thought that management research had some influence, but the greatest influence had been on other management academics including
what they currently research and will research and teach. On a five-
point scale (1 = very unimportant, to 5 = very important), the most
influence was on: Management theorizing – 3.91; Teaching – 3.63; Future research practice – 3.59; Management policy and practice in large
enterprises – 2.84; and Students' career decisions – 2.64. Despite Donald
Hambrick's (1994) plea, most respondents appeared to believe that the
Academy's research exercised little influence on broader social issues.

The qualitative data showed persistent themes of high concern
from senior scholars regarding the measures that institutions use to
gauge scholarly impact, effects on career development, management
research's value, and societal benefits. Most of the scholars stated that
the present system of faculty evaluation and business-school rankings
led to overreliance on more traditional techniques and methodologies,
and what journal editors find acceptable. Some scholars identified that
these developments had led to "junk science", journals as "incestuous
outlets for career-aspiring management academics", under reliance on
ideas, community and society, and excessive "balkanization" as management scholars became "angels dancing on a pin head". Some raised
concerns about the universal applicability and acceptance abroad of
U.S. faculty-evaluation standards and research approaches that diminish scholarly impact. One scholar categorized the spread of U.S.
research standards globally as amounting to "imperialism" and a
form of "colonialism", with disregard for context.

Management scholars made several actionable recommendations
on moving the field forward from its position of high academic legitimacy for wider social influence. Overall, to measure and to achieve
scholarly impact, the findings reinforced a need to develop composite
measures of scholarly impact, to reduce excessive focus on methodologies and techniques, to increase value placed on developing ideas important to external constituencies, and to introduce more applications
of theories to practice.

In conclusion, the AOM's report and findings fit into the larger
conversation on research and researchers' roles in society by exploring societal values and influence of research. The findings discussed
in subsequent chapters have relevance for the Academy's members,

universities' administrators, journal editors, tenure and promotion committees, accreditation agencies (e.g., AACSB, EQUIS), grant-giving organizations (e.g., NSF), policymakers, national reviews (e.g., PBRF, REF), and society at large.

References

Adetunji, O. O., & Renoe, S. D. (2017). Assessing broader impacts. *MRS Advances, 2*(31), 1681–1686.

Adler, N. J., & Harzing, A. W. (2009). When knowledge wins: Transcending the sense and nonsense of academic rankings. *Academy of Management Learning & Education, 8*(1), 72–95.

Amin, M., & Mabe, M. A. (2003) Impact factors: Use and abuse. *Medicina (B Aires), 63*(4), 347–354. PMID: 14518149.

Arnold, D. N., & Fowler, K. K. (2010). Nefarious numbers. *arXiv preprint arXiv:1010.0278.*

Biagioli, M., & Lippman, A. (Eds.). (2020). *Gaming the metrics: Misconduct and manipulation in academic research.* Cambridge, MA: MIT Press.

Borchardt, R., Moran, C., Cantrill, S., Chemjobber, Oh, S. A., & Hartings, M. R. (2018). Perception of the importance of chemistry research papers and comparison to citation rates. *PLoS ONE, 13*(3), e0194903. https://doi.org/10.1371/journal. pone.0194903

Brembs, B. (2018). Prestigious science journals struggle to reach even average reliability. *Frontiers in Human Neuroscience, 12,* 37.

Byrne, J. A. (2014) Cost of an academic article: $400K, *Poets & Quants,* July 14.

Callaway, E. (2016). Beat it, impact factor! Publishing elite turns against controversial metric. *Nature News, 535*(7611), 210.

Chavarro, D., Rafols, I., & Tang, P. (2017). To what extent is inclusion in the Web of Science an indicator of journal 'quality'? June 21. Available at SSRN: https://ssrn.com/abstract=2990653 or https://doi.org/10.2139/ssrn.2990653

Drucker, P. F. (1974). Tasks, responsibilities, practices. *New Yorks Row,* 121–122.

Garfield, E. (2006). The history and meaning of the Journal Impact Factor. *JAMA, 295*(1), 90–93. doi:10.1001/jama.295.1.90.

Haley, U. C. V., Page, M. C., Pitsis, T. S., Rivas, J. L., & Yu, K. F. (2017) Measuring and achieving scholarly impact: A report from the Academy of Management's Practice Theme Committee, Academy of Management, USA. doi:10.13140/RG.2.2.11747.86561.

Hambrick, D. C. (1994). What if the academy actually mattered? *Academy of Management Review, 19*(1), 11–16.

Lariviere, V., Kiermer, V., MacCallum, C. J., McNutt, M., Patterson, M., Pulverer, B., Swaminathan, S., Taylor, S., & Curry, S. (2016). A simple proposal for the publication of journal citation distributions. *BioRxiv, 062109.* https://doi.org/10.1101/062109

Lariviere, V., & Sugimoto, C. R. (2019). The journal impact factor: A brief history, critique, and discussion of adverse effects. In Glänzel, W., Moed,

H.F., Schmoch, U., & Thelwall, M. (eds.) *Springer handbook of science and technology indicators* (pp. 3–24). Cham, Switzerland: Springer.

McKiernan, E. C., Schimanski, L. A., Muñoz Nieves, C., Matthias, L., Niles, M. T., & Alperin, J. P. (2019) Use of the Journal Impact Factor in academic review, promotion, and tenure evaluations. *PeerJ Preprints, 7*, e27638v2. https://doi.org/10.7287/peerj.preprints.27638v2

McVeigh, M. E., & Mann, S. J. (2009). The journal impact factor denominator: Defining citable (counted) items. *Jama, 302*(10), 1107–1109.

O'Carroll, C., Rentier, B., Cabello Valdès, C., Esposito, F., Kaunismaa, E., Maas, K., Metcalfe, J., Vandevelde, K., Halleux, I., Kamerlin, C. L., & Lossau, N. (2017). *Evaluation of research careers fully acknowledging open science practices-rewards, incentives and/or recognition for researchers practicing Open Science.* Brusells: EU Publications. https://op.europa.eu/en/publication-detail/-/publication/47a3a330-c9cb-11e7-8e69-01aa75ed71a1

Research Excellence Framework (REF) (2021) https://www.ref.ac.uk/

Simkin, M. V., & Roychowdhury, V. P. (2002). Read before you cite!. *arXiv preprint cond-mat/0212043.*

Strathern, M. (1997). "'Improving ratings': Audit in the British University system". *European Review.* John Wiley & Sons, *5*(3), 305–321. doi:10.1002/(SICI)1234-981X(199707)5:3<305::AID-EURO184>3.0.CO;2-4.

Terwiesch, C., & Ulrich, K. T. (2014), Will video kill the classroom star? The threat and opportunity of massively open online courses for full-time MBA programs, The Wharton School, University of Pennsylvania, July 16, 2014.

Tort, A. B., Targino, Z. H., & Amaral, O. B. (2012). Rising publication delays inflate journal impact factors. *PLoS One, 7*(12), e53374.

Tsui, A. S. (2013). The spirit of science and socially responsible scholarship. *Management and Organization Review, 9*(3), 375–394.

Wahls, W. P. (2018). High cost of bias: Diminishing marginal returns on NIH grant funding to institutions, University of Arkansas for Medical Sciences. https://doi.org/10.1101/367847

Willmott, H. (2011). Journal list fetishism and the perversion of scholarship: Reactivity and the ABS list. *Organization, 18*(4), 429–442.

Yeung, A. W. (2017). Do neuroscience journals accept replications? A survey of literature. *Frontiers in Human Neuroscience, 11*, 468.

2 Why study scholarly impact

Usha C. V. Haley

This chapter begins with discussing the Practice Theme Committee's (PTC's) motivations and role in studying scholarly impact. Next, I explore definitions of impact in different regions of the world and diverse audiences; in our research, we defined scholarly impact as *"an auditable or recordable occasion of influence arising out of research"*. Finally, I identify how we structured the Academy of Management (AOM) study on scholarly impact.

2.1 Motivations for the study

The narrative contestation over the demonstration, valuation, and assessment of academic and scholarly impact (Sandhu et al., 2019), coupled with growing concerns over diminished relevance of management scholarship to practice (Aguinis et al., 2020), has assumed great importance and relevance for the AOM's members. The PTC proposed an AOM Strategic Doing project to achieve the following outcomes under the strategic intent of Professional Impact: (1) engaging our colleagues and relevant stakeholders in reflexive consideration and conversation about the meaning and sensemaking of scholarly impact and for whom, followed by conversation that broadens current measurements of impact beyond articles, citations, or media mentions; (2) drawing on the findings of an all-Academy survey and knowledge-dissemination workshops to identify resources in which the AOM may invest to address members' research, teaching, and training needs to achieve scholarly impact. Simply stated, this project aimed to provide the AOM's leadership and members with both a mirror and window to comprehend better the complex, pluralistic nature of scholarly impact, including how the AOM's direct stakeholders (members) and indirect

DOI: 10.4324/9780429298981-2

stakeholders (e.g., governments, university administrators, managers, and policymakers) value and comprehend this impact.

As an all-Academy Committee, the PTC was charged to "raise the visibility of management practice as an important professional focus within the Academy of Management" and to "encourage the Academy to become exposed to and provide exposure for application-oriented professional-development opportunities". With this report, the PTC suggested ways that the AOM's scholars, academic institutions, and regulatory bodies may measure the impact of research in societal contexts around the world; we also hoped to identify avenues for more practice-relevant scholarship that would enhance research, put knowledge into action, and thereby achieve scholarly impact. The project highlighted our discipline's broader role and social mission, including its place in the ecosystem of economic, political, and social ideas and actions.

We hoped that through the knowledge this project produced, the AOM would move to the global forefront of understanding and driving responses to the impact agenda. **Appendix 1** lists those who contributed their ideas, time, and suggestions on the scholarly impact project over two years. The PTC's report (AOM, 2018) received attention beyond the AOM, with discussions at major accreditation bodies (e.g., the AACSB), in major academic journals (e.g., the *Academy of Management Journal*), in blogs (e.g., *LSE's Impact of Social Sciences*), and in other venues (see *BizEd*, 2018; Haley, 2018; Simsek et al., 2018; Bisoux, 2019). The conversation continues.

2.2 What is impact?

Understandings of the term impact differ between users and audiences (see Penfield et al., 2014). Distinctions exist between academic impact or the intellectual contribution to one's field of study within academia, and external socioeconomic impact beyond academia. As Penfield et al. (2014) identified, in the United Kingdom, evaluation of academic and broader socioeconomic impact takes place separately with impact as meaning research influence beyond academia. Such a distinction does not exist in U.S. institutions, for the most part. In our study, we defined Scholarly Impact as *"an auditable or recordable occasion of influence arising out of research"*.

Between a third and two-fifths of all research originates from the social sciences; as we discussed in the previous chapter, external stakeholders such as governmental funding and ratings bodies have insisted that scholars conduct more research that matters to practice. In management, despite a desire to encourage external impact through research, the study revealed that our institutions appeared to reward behaviors that thwarted what we hoped to achieve (for a discussion of the phenomenon of rewarding A while hoping for B, please see Kerr, 1975). Indeed, despite the flurry of articles on scholarly impact (see **Figure 1.1**), limited agreement existed between what the AOM's members regarded as scholarly impact and how institutions measured it.

We also had an interest in noticing differences and similarities in regional perceptions and effectiveness of policies on scholarly impact. Other researchers (Ràfols et al., 2015) have shown how including or excluding journals from the Web of Science (WoS), Scopus, and CABI databases affects research topics' coverage and accessibility. For example, CABI had a much higher coverage of the issue "rice" (77 percent) than Scopus (60 percent) or WoS (43 percent). Research emphases and stakeholders' interests differed as well with WoS and Scopus focusing on molecular biology, traditional genetics, and industry-related consumption, and CABI focusing on productivity, plant nutrition, plant characteristics, and plant protection. WoS and Scopus related their research interests to seed companies' and the food industry's interests, while CABI related to local farmers' and local communities' interests.

Prior research has shown that one-size evaluation instruments rarely fit all circumstances, countries, and institutions, resulting in socially, economically, and environmentally irrelevant research and potential misuses of scant resources for many third-world countries. Dangers from these prestigious databases included value-based hierarchies, concentrations of recognition, and marginalizations of pressing challenges for many countries and stakeholders. Consequently, we assumed that research evaluations should show sensitivity to context and to account for diversity in scientific production (related to geography, language, discipline, and other factors) to overcome the deficiencies of conventional, evaluation practices.

2.3 Structuring the study

The project consisted of two interrelated parts: a qualitative study and quantitative survey on scholarly impact and its meaning to the AOM's various stakeholders. Specifically, our findings dealt with how the AOM's membership defines and measures scholarly impact and identifies key external constituencies. In this fashion, we hoped to contribute to a clear, comprehensive, and less-contaminated definition of scholarly impact than any currently available, with implications for the field's future development.

We adopted a preliminary, qualitative approach to understanding scholarly impact before engaging with any larger-scale, quantitative study: we assumed that a more grounded understanding of the meaning of scholarly impact would enhance the value of a quantitative, survey approach. To understand the issues that surrounded scholarly impact, we began through open-ended, in-depth interviews with 30 of the AOM's distinguished members who had held leadership positions in the organization; for an in-depth understanding of the themes, we narrowed this sample down to ten. Our sample for the qualitative interviews included seven Fellows of the AOM (Professors Sir Cary Cooper, Thomas Cummings, William Guth, Ian Mitroff, Karlene Roberts, Howard Thomas, and Anne Tsui), two former Presidents of the AOM (Professors Thomas Cummings and Anne Tsui), the founding chair of the Business Policy and Strategy (BPS) division (Professor Guth), a founder of Organizations and the Natural Environment (ONE) (Professor Mitroff), former chairs of the Management Education Development (MED) division (Professor Sir Cooper), Research Methods (RM) division (Professor Boje), Managerial and Organizational Cognition (MOC) division (Professor Ashkanasy), and Management Consulting (MC) division (Professor Bonnet). These academics had published in and edited the major academically oriented Management journals including *Academy of Management Review, Academy of Management Journal, Administrative Science Quarterly, Strategic Management Journal, Academy of Management Learning & Education, Organization Science, Management Science, Organization Studies, Journal of International Business Studies, Journal of Management Studies, Journal of Organizational Behavior,* and *Journal of Applied Psychology.* The sample had also published in practitioner-related outlets such as the *Harvard Business Review* and *California Management Review,* had written op-eds and scholarly as well as best-selling books, and had achieved demonstrably wide reach beyond academics through their research.

The sample for our qualitative interviews spanned the AOM's myriad divisions and interest groups, including but not limited to: BPS, Critical Management Studies (CMS), Entrepreneurship (ENT), Human Resources (HR), International Management (IM), MOC, MC, MED, Management Spirituality and Religion (MSR), Organization Development and Change (ODC), Organization and Management Theory (OMT), Organizational Behavior (OB), ONE, RM, and Social Issues in Management (SIM). The sample covered all the AOM's geographic regions of membership (including North America, Asia,

South America, Australia/New Zealand, the United Kingdom/Europe, and Africa) and included several members with senior administrative experience in these regions.

The qualitative study and subsequent all-Academy survey explored how the AOM's various stakeholders (including faculty, administrators, and regulators) viewed measures of external impact. We also ascertained the independence of different measures through statistical approaches. In the qualitative research, to identify the stakeholders on which management scholars might want to have an impact and the types of influence desired, we built on the preliminary conceptual approach that the AOM Board of Governors' Professional Impact Strategic Committee developed in 2014–2015. We used this qualitative understanding and the sample's narratives of scholarly impact to build a survey that we distributed to the AOM's members. **Appendix 2** presents the electronic survey that we distributed to a random sample of the AOM's members.

The ensuing chapters discuss some of the qualitative and quantitative analyses that we undertook. Institutions, history, and past strategic investments influenced concerns about scholarly impact, and these characteristics differed across the major regions from which the AOM draws its membership. We also undertook geographic analysis of differences and similarities in the results for North America, Latin America, Africa/Middle East, Asia, Europe, and Oceania. Our results show that despite many similarities, members defined several aspects of scholarly impact differently across geographic regions; consequently, a single framework may not apply globally. The final chapter presents recommendations for measuring and achieving scholarly impact.

References

Academy of Management (2018). Strategic plan – Scholarly impact report. https://aom.org/about-aom/strategic-plan/scholarly-impact-report

Aguinis, H., Cummings, C., Ramani, R. S., & Cummings, T. G. (2020). "An A is an A": The new bottom line for valuing academic research. *Academy of Management Perspectives*, *34*(1), 135–154.

Bisoux, T. (2019) A new era for business research, *BizEd Magazine*, AACSB International, October 30. https://bized.aacsb.edu/articles/2019/november/a-new-era-for-business-research

BizEd (2018). The essence of scholarly impact, Research+Insights, *BizEd Magazine*, March/April, pp. 10–11. https://bized.aacsb.edu/articles/2018/03/the-essence-of-scholarly-impact

Haley, U. C. V. (2018). Beyond impact factors: An Academy of Management report on measuring scholarly impact, LSE Social Impact blog, March 2.

https://blogs.lse.ac.uk/impactofsocialsciences/2018/03/02/beyond-impact-factors-an-academy-of-management-report-on-measuring-scholarly-impact/

Kerr, S. (1975). On the folly of rewarding A, while hoping for B. *Academy of Management Journal, 18*(4), 769–783.

Penfield, T., Baker, M. J., Scoble, R., & Wykes, M. C. (2014). Assessment, evaluations, and definitions of research impact: A review. *Research Evaluation, 23*(1), 21–32.

Ràfols, I., Ciarli, T., & Chavarro, D. (2015). Under-reporting research relevant to local needs in The Global South. Database biases in the representation of knowledge on Rice. *ISSI.* doi:10.13039/501100000269 Corpus ID: 11720845

Sandhu, S., Perera, S., & Sardeshmukh, S. R. (2019). Charted courses and meandering trails: Crafting success and impact as Business School Academics. *Academy of Management Learning & Education, 18*(2), 153–185.

Simsek, Z., Bansal, P., Shaw, J. D., Heugens, P., & Smith, W. K. (2018). From the editors—Seeing practice impact in new ways. *Academy of Management Journal, 61*(6), 2021–2025.

3 Qualitative data, analysis, and results

Usha C. V. Haley

This chapter begins with a discussion on methodology and sampling. The author then describes the analysis and highlights key results.

3.1 Sampling & methodology

The first stage of our research identified the issues relating to scholarly impact of most interest to the Academy of Management's (AOM's) membership. In consultation with Professors Gayle Baugh (liaison to the Practice Theme Committee), Tyrone Pitsis, and Kuo Frank Yu (members of the AOM's Strategic Development Initiative, see Academy of Management, 2018), we identified a non-probability sample of 30 impactful and historically influential AOM members (Giddens, 1990; Ziman, 2000; Creswell, 2007). This initial pass included open-ended questions to identify the Who, What, When, Where, Why, and How of scholarly impact which through interviews and focus groups would spotlight areas for subsequent narrative analysis (DeWalt & DeWalt, 2002).

This first round of data collection identified a data-saturation point of about ten respondents (Delbecq et al., 1975; Seidman, 1991). We concluded that a sample of ten would then prove sufficient for further in-depth narrative and thematic analysis (Barad, 2007; Baker & Edwards, 2012). Usha Haley subsequently conducted in-depth, semi-structured, personal interviews with ten of the sample, including all members that the AOM's Board of Governors identified as having substantial impact in the field of Management. The Board of Governors chose the interviewees on criteria including very high citations, leadership roles in the Academy (e.g., President, Division Head, Academy Fellow), leadership roles in their institutions (e.g., Deans, Provosts), leadership roles as editors of major journals (e.g., *Academy of Management Journal, Strategic Management Journal, Academy of Management Learning &*

DOI: 10.4324/9780429298981-3

Education, Journal of Organizational Behavior), and leadership roles in regulatory bodies (e.g., AACSB, REF). Professor Haley conducted all personal interviews by phone or over Skype and interviewees verified written transcripts for accuracy of content; most interviews lasted 45 minutes to an hour (Court & Abbas, 2013; Deakin & Wakefield, 2014).

To examine the lived experience of this smaller sample (Barad, 2007; van Manen, 2016), Professor Haley conducted phenomenological interviews that focused on their own experiences and the meanings they made of that experience (Villa, 2017). These descriptions formed the basis of the reconstructed interpretations or manifestations of scholarly impact for later quantitative inquiry (Vagle, 2018). Qualitative data thereby provided a richer description of the opportunities and constraints for scholarly impact than we could accomplish with numbers alone (Benney & Hughes, 1956; Briggs, 1986; Bamberger, 2018; Lofland et al., 2016).

3.2 Analysis of qualitative data and findings

For the thematic data analysis (Denzin & Lincoln, 2011), the author generated initial codes based on judgment and automated coding of text (Leximancer) to generate labels for recurring patterns. The labels thereby attached categorical meanings to bits of text to represent single concepts, even though specific examples differed from each other. The analysis sometimes gave single bits of text several codes to emphasize different parts, or to represent different interpretations of the same parts. To control for her subjective judgments and researcher's bias, Professor Haley conducted iterative coding with the Strategic Development Team's input (with Professors Melanie Page, Tyrone Pitsis, and Frank Yu).

We coded the qualitative data for specific information on what could and should constitute measures of scholarly impact, as well as for suggestions for the AOM on possible avenues to increase the discipline's impact. The results show persistent themes of high concern from impactful scholars regarding the measures that institutions use to gauge scholarly impact, effects on career development, Management research's value, and societal benefits. **Table 3.1** highlights key points from each interview.

Most of the scholars stated that the present system of faculty evaluation and business-school rankings had led to an over-reliance on techniques, methodologies, and what journals' editors may find acceptable. Some scholars identified that these developments in evaluations and rankings had led to "junk science", journals as "incestuous

Table 3.1 Phenomenological Interviews on Measuring Scholarly Impact[1]

Name	Impact Factors and Citations	Journal Articles and Rankings	Books and Reports	Better Measures	Faculty Evaluations	Big Problems	Recommendations for AOM
Scholar 1 (UK)	"Thomson Reuters Impact factors are less important for me as a measure of research impact than 'how has my research influenced government policy in my country or business community'"?	"A major downside to our focus on 4*publications [is] they tend to be very technical, and not problem focused. They make an incremental contribution, but, in the most part, have little impact. They are far too idiosyncratic to appeal to broader audiences… Across all the Academy journals in any year,	"We do not value books, which can be used to develop ideas with real implications, and therefore have the potential for broader impact… Most importantly, books are very important for a policy and business focus and impact… One of the great contributions of books is the ability to explore a topic	"We should be encouraging applied research, and not just 4* journal standards. Although science in the real world is far more sloppy and less controllable, the impact benefits are much greater… Being an editor of a journal is not impact. The question to be asked is how has your research affected business policy and practice or changed government policy and practice? Economics is the most successful social science when it comes	"People orient their work towards what gets tenure. So, in the field of Management, we tend not to research real-life problems, do not work enough with governments, and do not publish in vehicles that influence business policy and practice…We do have vehicles that reach managers, but these do not count for much in the academic evaluation of an individual's research record. Even HBR would be evaluated less	"Our aim should be doing research that influences business policy and practice and government policy and practice. But, overwhelmingly our focus is on incremental, highly-technical research, which doesn't translate easily into impact…We do not do enough as academics to have impact…In my experience, very few academics talk to governments and change government	"The US model of publishing has become very influential globally. It would be wonderful if AOM changed the focus of their journals to encourage people to do more meaningful research that could make a real contribution to practice and policy in business and government, and avoid the trap of being an incestuous outlet for career-aspiring management academics… In my opinion, AMJ needs to

(Continued)

Name	Impact Factors and Citations	Journal Articles and Rankings	Books and Reports	Better Measures	Faculty Evaluations	Big Problems	Recommendations for AOM
Scholar 1 (continued)		probably only 2 or 3 articles may make any real impact. These journals and their research is mostly focused on other academics".	in depth. It is not telegraphic as so many journal articles are, where the implications for policy or practice are rarely explored… Unfortunately, books are not taken seriously in promotion and tenure, but their contribution is invaluable".	to influencing policy, and we can learn a great deal from [it]… We have a real dilemma in the social sciences generally. We are concerned about a lack of influence on policy, yet A+ journal articles cannot be the only thing we do and value. Publications in magazines and newspapers should count as well… If you look at our Academy articles, the implications for changing government policy or even business policy and practice is	strongly than a 4* journal. Yet, it has the potential to influence business policy and practice… How do you make an impact if your promotion is based on 4* publications which are designed for other academics rather than business or government or NGOs?… Senior people after getting tenure should concentrate doing and mentoring the value-added of their work on	policy…Even our practitioner journals, HBR, CMR, tend on balance to influence practice rather than policy. So, a 2x2 matrix can help enable good business practice, but this influence, in my view, tends to be transitory… Influencing governments is very important. We have become too focused on methodology – and not so much on is there a real-	refocus its energies and judge articles not only on their scholarly contribution and methodology, but on the impact it makes to policy and practice. It is orientated too much to other aspiring, tenure-seeking academics rather than its impact in the real world of policy and practice. Being able to analyse data via the most sophisticated statistical techniques

Scholar 1 (continued)				"very limited, although in recent years we are developing some AOM journals that may deliver the impact agenda in the future. For real impact, we must influence policy, both governmental and in business strategy".	policy and practice. Our senior professors should lead the way. Stop obsessing with publishing in 4* journals. Senior professors should encourage junior faculty to publish books, write for practitioner-oriented journals, etc. But, people do not want to muddy the water".	life problem that needs resolution. We should be asking: what is the best research we can do under the circumstances to influence policy or practice?"	should not be the primary objective of any journal; it should be what contribution it makes to business, society and policy... I would like to see AOM journals require a major section of an article on implications for government and business policy and practice".
Scholar 2 (USA)	"Citations, including [Clarivate's Journal] Impact factors, are absolutely not a measure of impact. They should	"Publishing in A plus journals has of course increased in importance. B-Schools have to compete on the same criteria. They bend	"Books would win hands down for impact on practice. Almost no managers that I know reads our journal articles, but all read books that	"We can use proxy measures... Citations are a proxy measure but they are subject to abuse...do not measure impact on practice...	"From Assistant to Associate, I would place 100% weight on writing articles for top-ranked journals. From Associate to Full Professor a greater	"The link between scholarly research and practice is unattended to. Economists say that this is not a B-School issue. They say that there	"The AOM should continue to do what it seems to be doing with this project. It sounds like it is trying to broaden the meaning of impact beyond

(Continued)

Name	Impact Factors and Citations	Journal Articles and Rankings	Books and Reports	Better Measures	Faculty Evaluations	Big Problems	Recommendations for AOM
Scholar 2 (continued)	be labelled for what they are – measures of citations. Labelling them as Impact is an abuse of the English language".	to citation indices. They can count citations and you do not have to be too smart to do this. B-Schools are saying the better we do on citations, the better we are. I don't think too many in the market are paying attention".	can impact management and practice... can help in the development of applied theories...can also help other academics to improve the ability of theories to predict experience".	[Appropriate] measures include not just citations but also keynote speeches, expert witness testimonies and the like. But B-Schools have locked into impact as scholarly research. Not many practitioners read our research and I do not think even many academics do".	proportion of the evaluation, perhaps 50%, should be paid to activities that may impact practice".	is a built-in incentive within the system for consultants and managers to read scholarly articles and to translate them. But, no one I know sees an incentive in doing this translation. So, the chasm between practice and theory building/ testing is getting wider".	pure citations and provide mechanisms for support of other activities. Other than what you are doing [Usha, and these activities[PTC], I do not see much change in AOM presentations. I do not see more practitioners showing up to listen to AOM presentations. But, through this project the AOM shows that it is aware of concerns and issues and. is ready to examine them. However, real commitment to doing something [to change the status quo] is yet to be seen at this point"

Scholar 3 (USA)							
Scholar 3 (USA)	"No [I do not think [Clarivate's Journal] Impact figures are an adequate measure of impact]. A particular journal's impact factor is not a measure of impact… The incentive system at the university level has an impact on journals… If universities want their faculty to publish in journals with	"Individuals and universities seek to establish reputation, certainly, but use counts in top journals as the primary indicator. Universities incentivize people not to do long-term projects with potential for impact, but emphasize 'do-able' incremental projects—ones with probably certain results. I don't know many people who don't	"Books are incredibly important, yet faculty members, especially junior faculty, are discouraged from writing books. Yet, some of the richest theoretical ideas come from books. Books give a researcher room to explore new theory or explore particular contexts in complex ways. Books written for practitioner audiences can potentially have incredible impact, but I can't imagine	"We have impact through our students and through our teaching. That can be good and bad. There are ideas in textbooks that are sticky, but not necessarily that well supported in research, but still, our influence in the classroom matters…We influence our students through core concepts and theories that we cover [and that they later use]".	"Our evaluation systems are imperiling external impact and incentivizing the wrong behaviors. I do not believe in a system of promotion and tenure in which we've lost sight of why concepts such as academic freedom and tenure even exist. The ideal is… The purpose of higher education institutions as 'conducted for the common good and not to further the interest of either the individual	"In education, we are becoming keenly aware of the impact of high-stakes measurement systems at every level. At the K-12 level the concern is that the focus on test scores may in the long run undermine the goal of creating a love of learning. I see the decision by universities to use a narrow measurement of impact (citation rates, numbers of publications, and journal impact factors) as having	"I have recommended that the AOM establish a website for teaching. The AOM needs to think about creating a portal to have an impact on teaching and practice, to reach managers. We find ways to talk directly about theory and research in creative ways, to make our theories accessible to students and practitioners. In this way, we make our ideas

(Continued)

Name	Impact Factors and Citations	Journal Articles and Rankings	Books and Reports	Better Measures	Faculty Evaluations	Big Problems	Recommendations for AOM
Scholar 3 (continued)	high impact factors, journals need high impact factors to attract submissions. This can create incentives for journal editors to attempt to manipulate the impact factor by virtue of the types of papers they might publish, and some authors have reported pressure to cite the journal in revisions. Then to counter this	know of or haven't used the term 'quick hit'. That's not exactly a code term for 'impact'".	those actually getting counted in any but the most incidental way….Textbooks remain an important part of education, particularly at the undergraduate level. Some can be slow to adopt new research, and can retain material that may no longer be useful. They also tend to downplay differences and paradigmatic diversity. Still, to the extent that a textbook creates a strong narrative, that story can influence student		teacher or the institution as a whole' [as stated in] AAUP 1940. It is not clear how our numbers of articles, journal rankings, citations and other metrics used to demonstrate individual impact and university reputation quite reach this 'common good' ideal. In fact, the quantification process has choked impact. It is [an] almost classic goal displacement… Even within departments, numbers of citations and the impact factor of	narrowed our concept of impact and how to achieve it. At the same time, it has created other negative side effects in the broader system of teaching and research".	comprehensible and even inspiring. We are taking small steps – AMJ has developed a website in which researchers talk about their work, and the new Discoveries journal is using multimedia to bring their papers to life. But our research world remains relatively insulated. We need to take a far more active approach to closing the gap between research and practice. It cannot be up to the individual researcher to do so. This seems like an important

| Scholar 3 (continued) | perception, editors may not recommend citation of an important paper when it clearly should be. Both are perversions that do not serve development of good research". | perspectives after they leave school, even if details might be lost. This puts a burden on textbook authors and faculty adopters, but that reality should guide their choices. The importance also asks us to hold publishers to care about the ideal of 'long-term impact'. | journals in which faculty members publish are now important to promotion and tenure decisions, rather than peer faculty review of the research… For faculty evaluations we need to ask, does the instructor bring the most recent research into the classroom? Does the instructor inspire application of theories and concepts? We tend to look at behaviors that affect student attention, [to] discrete learning outcomes, and ask students to judge | function the Academy of Management might take on. I would love to see that happen. The model might be the "white papers" that you see on the websites of some consulting firms. The Academy has done a good job of promoting certain high-profile papers to the press. I think something more permanent in the way of outreach would be terrific… The weight of routines and material practices at the university level is significant. The Academy of Management could have an effect on how |

(Continued)

Name	Impact Factors and Citations	Journal Articles and Rankings	Books and Reports	Better Measures	Faculty Evaluations	Big Problems	Recommendations for AOM
Scholar 3 (continued)					satisfaction with the instructor. We need to ask has the student become more motivated to learn in the long run? Our metrics and 'learning outcomes' orientation may be a factor that focuses instructors on short-term performance that is measurable at the end of a class".		impact is defined, perhaps showing how concepts of impact can expand beyond those routines (citations, impact factors, and numbers of articles). We need to act collectively with other academic organizations in Marketing, Finance, Operations, Accounting and others if this is our goal, however. Something more systemic is likely required".
Scholar 4 (USA)		"AACSB should get out of outcome assessment. AACSB accreditation efforts have resulted in		"Scholarly impact should deal with reaching real corporations and real people who need our help. Scholarly impact is not a new way	"When I evaluate professors for full, I get 3 types of packages: First, Type A with really high-level, ranked journal	"AACSB outcome assessment has done to academia what has been done to doctors and nurses. Too much	"I would advise that we widen our zone of participation outside technical specialists in academic

Scholar 4 (continued)

ranking of journals which is bad and hurts the production of new ideas... New ideas are not generated in ranked journals which are unreadable. You cannot reach people through esoteric language. ASQ started as a readable journal with lay people contributing and changed as it became more prestigious".

of measuring error variance... All vehicles mentioned [in AOM survey] for scholarly impact are important. Teaching in EMBA programs should not deal with regurgitating old familiar models – but, translating complex materials for professionals is important".

publications, great teaching and great service. Second, Type B packages with few journals, not well cited, but great impact with books, testimonies, associations, speeches, so they made a huge impact. Type B is equally important. Third, Type C with no impact in journals or socio-economic space. This is the sad case. Type A and Type B should be equally positioned in any evaluation".

paperwork and everyone is obsessed with being either reaccredited or being sued. Students are not a key priority in any institution... In terms of targets of influence, I would rank them as: (1) corporations, (2) governments, (3) NGOs and government organizations, (4) students, and (5) lastly academics... So many things are wrong with this system. Working with real people should be the most important vehicle, and the least important

fields to people actually on the firing line. Our ideas take years to come to fruition, but if you do not participate with real people it is useless. You need partnering relationships... We have a schizophrenic system that has failed...Public advocacy is important. But our advice for new scholars is on how to play the journal-ranking game not how to make a difference. This is a big mistake. Students leave here trying to fit into narrow little blocks

(Continued)

Name	Impact Factors and Citations	Journal Articles and Rankings	Books and Reports	Better Measures	Faculty Evaluations	Big Problems	Recommendations for AOM
Scholar 4 (continued)						should be refereed journal articles…".	to get a job. The practice is rooted in the Academy of Management placement system".
Scholar 5 (France)	"To do impactful research, one should have an eye on the relationship between the will to change things and how our actions impact reality. These issues should impact performance appraisal – not just results in terms of publications and impact factors".	"A plus journals have increased in importance and this is both good and bad. There is an increasing isomorphism in what is published. This raises the standards of debate and discussion. But the bad is there is not much diversity. Qualifications of what constitutes an A plus journal [have] also become		"I used and argued for multiple criteria to evaluate academic research. These criteria included not just research issues. On research, I would typically look at publications, but also the ability to translate the publications for managers – the dissemination of that research. Did they have another version of the paper for a business journal for example?	"When evaluating faculty, one has to balance between senior faculty with the confidence and [established] habits of publishing and junior faculty with fresh ideas. But, in Europe, the junior faculty have become socialized in the American way of publishing. Young scholars know how to publish. They know the tricks. In Europe, senior faculty	"Scholarly society has become a bit more open, and there are many efforts for Europeans and Asians to come into the game. But, it is still an American game. Some communities can get included in the American game. For example, EURAM has a call for papers modelled on the AOM, dates, peer review, pages, etc. It has taken its	"I am not sure about what AOM could do about the impact of business schools compared to AACSB which has views on B-school strategy. Maybe, AOM could do something about publications and calculating impact factors. There is something obviously not going well in publishing. Once an article

| Scholar 5 (continued) | an issue. Publications have become a game. For example, the *Journal of Business Ethics* has many issues in a year, making it a reachable target and a highly ranked journal. Ideas and community have become less important". | Did they make presentations of their ideas to professional congresses and give speeches to professionals? What are their academic networks, scientific associations and responsibility for communities? So, I look at the Quality of Publications + the Quality of Dissemination. Within the research, I look at more than just where the paper was published. What are the papers about? What position did they take? I look at the way in which the research takes in context elements. | of 50 or 60 have not been trained in the American way of publishing. The AOM should look at seniority in a different way in the US and other countries. Senior European faculty may not be trained in American ways of publishing research, but they have good ideas. Also, these faculty have been trained in their own language, French or whatever. They do not have the same research and writing style as in the US. Some local researchers are never translated into English. References and | conference to the level of the American game. EGOS is similar... This is not easy. It is difficult to play the same relational game – who is important, who is to be cited". | is published, one cannot do anything more with it, cannot distribute it freely, cannot use the data. The profit motives of the publishing industry have affected our profession and prevent us from participating freely in the scholar conversation... This is a very good idea to include European colleges in this AOM survey. We have a different view point as we try to keep pace". |

(Continued)

Name	Impact Factors and Citations	Journal Articles and Rankings	Books and Reports	Better Measures	Faculty Evaluations	Big Problems	Recommendations for AOM
Scholar 5 (continued)				Ideas are more important than methodology. Reality is important... For impactful research, colleagues should be able to develop ideas that can be implemented in companies – not just methodologies. The ideas should have an impact on business life".	citations become an issue. We lose a lot".		
Scholar 6 (Singapore)	"Rankings funnel people into a citation game. Citations are important. But, there is a real market for more applied research. But that is not as highly	"Yes, A plus journals have increased in importance. [Business School] Deans say well I need to get programs ranked.... [Concentrating on A journals] is not the way	"Books are important for scholarly impact – not textbooks which should be examined in pedagogical context. [Books] allow one to posit a new view. These books do not necessarily have	"Scholarship is about working out the incentives to do impactful research. But, there are no incentives to do inter-disciplinary research.... To measure impact, we have to go beyond citation measures and	"One gets tenure and promotion with high citations, relatively good teaching and no impact on the management profession. Some people leap across and actually have some impact.	"Some people become Deans because they get paid more. Then they become more conservative. Business schools have become less about management education and more about	"The areas of interest at SMS and AOM are also becoming narrower and narrower. We have balkanized interest groups...[we have become] like angels dancing on a pin head. Look

Scholar 6
(continued)

regarded as the top journals as they don't [translate directly] into rankings".

to develop scholarship... Younger people are being pushed into publishing in A journals – but the [research] focus has become narrower and narrower...We measure impact by number of articles in A journals – but this is minimal impact. We must have 2000 [recent] abstracts on methodology alone...Editorial policies have stifled scholarly impact. Editorial policies are so narrow. JMS

to be scholarly monographs. JC Spender did that with his doctoral dissertation on industry recipes. Rumelt did so as well. Consulting reports are important if they have longer time horizons as they show application".

impact factors of journals. We could use several alternative measures: (1) Downloads, such as at Researchgate. Does anyone read the bloody thing? (2) We could also look at downloads and reads on SSRN. In Finance and Economics, these measures count as much as a B+/A journal... To measure scholarly impact, we should ask: Has any of this research been published in applied journals? Have the researchers had any impact on organizations? If they provide download

But, we have no incentives as deans to encourage these people... Questions we should ask [for promotion and tenure] are: What have you done that is an interesting area of research? Where do you see this going? How do you develop as a career academic? But, we have an isomorphism of accreditation agencies which reinforce and mandate the P&T system".

being a cash cow. We are illegitimate in research profiles at universities... We pursue rankings. As Rakesh Khurana indicated we are all subject to the "tyranny of the rankings". Rankings such as FT and UT Dallas push towards ROIs and [short-term] profits from research... Outside the USA, many academics are no way close to publishing in an A journal, but they are good at management education. We need to include these indicators as well. US

at all the OB and IO interest groups. This balkanization serves as a barrier to scholarship. The impact of our research is on a very narrow segment. My recommendation to the AOM is let us not get too balkanized. There are too many Interest Groups. The AOM is too bloody large. It's like a pharma convention. It has become a meat market for younger people to sell their wares to potential employers. The incentive systems are not aligned [to

(Continued)

Name	Impact Factors and Citations	Journal Articles and Rankings	Books and Reports	Better Measures	Faculty Evaluations	Big Problems	Recommendations for AOM
Scholar 6 (continued)		is far more eclectic than AMJ or AMR. [Scholars and editors] put a paper in a template, so intensely boring. Most of these papers are cures for insomnia".		[statistics], who is downloading their articles? Who is citing their work? Is it just other academics? We need to ask how is the research used? Who is looking? Let us list the top 50 management thinkers: do they have impact and why?…We need to count research grants [which are more interdisciplinary]".		schools have engaged in imperialism and colonialism – this is the best way [they say] without looking at the context and culture that generates good managers. The US and the West is not the norm. We are supposed to be global educators".	do impactful scholarship]. Until you get tenure you produce in high-quality journals. There is no incentive to do impactful research. There is no incentive to do inter-disciplinary research even after tenure. The journals are too narrow".
Scholar 7 (Australia)	"[Clarivate Journal Impact Factors are] important to ascertain scholarly impact. In Australia, we also pay attention to Scopus. UQ	"A plus journals have become more important, first because they establish the reputation of the school for research. Second, because you can attract		"The focus is external in Australia. You cannot have an academic career here if you do not have an international focus. You have to travel. You have to develop and maintain	"Citations are the major measure of scholarly impact – for an academic it is important that other academics pay attention. But, industry contacts, industry roles and teaching		"For the AOM, they should know that for countries like Australia and New Zealand, the international impact we have is all important. A profile at the Academy is very

| Scholar 7 (continued) | Authors' statistics is an internal measure we use... We also have the ARC-sponsored ERA (Excellence in Research in Australia) for evaluation – for management, not based on citation data... but on peer evaluation of publications. But, if you publish in a high-ranking journal, your research is evaluated more favorably... Impact factors are not ideal | an international profile...Grant money is an indication of having external impact. You have two types of Australian Research Council grants – basic and applied. Basic grants are quite difficult to get, but applied grants are done with industry contacts and, once a substantial cash contribution is secured, are much easier... We may not need new measures of scholarly impact. Google Scholar is becoming more sophisticated. It's my first port of call. It helps if an academic gets a Google Scholar profile. | should also play an important part in evaluations. ...In Australia, the more senior the position, the higher the expectations of scholarly impact. For the highest level, Professor, you would be expected to have success with top-tier journals and grant-writing success... External impact is demonstrated through getting grant money and more. For Associate Professor and Professor positions you have to demonstrate extensive external impact. There are cases where faculty | important for an Australian academic. Some look at EGOS and European academic organizations, and others like me, at the AOM". |
| | faculty confident that they can publish at that level... Australia uses a much wider list than many in the US. [Our university] has dropped its own list and adopted the ABDC (Australian Business Dean's Council list) as one of our faculty chaired the committee... [Our Business School] also has an in-house star-plus list and we give $15,000 of research funding for any article published on that list. The money goes | | | |

(Continued)

Name	Impact Factors and Citations	Journal Articles and Rankings	Books and Reports	Better Measures	Faculty Evaluations	Big Problems	Recommendations for AOM
Scholar 7 (continued)	measurements and they can be improved. There is subjectivity. They are flawed. And, there is selectivity. I have been cited as an example of how not to do research. My opinion pieces have been cited to bolster others' opinions... But citations and impact factors are the best we have at the moment".	into a research fund. The usual suspects are on that list plus JOB, JAP. We also have a star list which is the other A and A plus journals [in] ABDC – for that we give $6,000 and $10,000 respectively for an article. [A competing] Business School gives $45,000 research funding for any article published in the FT45".		Harzing's Publish or Perish was good too but has been seriously wounded by Google Scholar's decision not to include a discipline identifier".	got promotion to the full Professor level through showing impact at the government or society level".		"I see this project as very encouraging. We need to look at our mission
Scholar 8 (USA)	"Yes, we use some of that [Clarivate's Journal Impact	"We debate these lists as a faculty. A lot of thought and discussion goes into it"	"We do not have a lot of books coming out of [our Business School]. But	"My ideal measure of scholarly impact would be some combination of	"To get tenure, you need A publications and we have lists developed by the	"We have a debate going around in schools – we look like a discipline	

| Scholar 8 (continued) | Factors]. But, it is possible to have a high impact factor and not be considered an A journal. The *Journal of Management* with a very high impact is such an example. We do not consider it an A journal, but just under an A. We have discussed this. Historically, we do not see this as a mainstream journal". | purely academic books count. Warren Bennis's book would not count and would be seen as textbook. We would count academic press books such as Oxford University Press and Cambridge University Press". | citations among academics and notoriety in a larger audience. Herman Aguinis wrote an article where he looked at Google citations [mentions] as a measure of scholarly impact. But the Google citations were to the applied and not to the academic articles. So some combination of Google mentions, outer impact and academic citations would provide a [better] measure of scholarly impact". | departments. We are looking to see if you have carved out a niche in the area. … We are discipline based, so you can publish only in Psych journals for example and get tenure in our Management department. For tenure to full, we want discipline-based and management research which is more applied. Yes, it is mostly about publications but you also have to [have the ability] to teach – we are a private school. We have lists of A journals for every department and subunit. In our | but we are a professional school. We have worked our way into a corner and I see no good coming out of this. We forget we are a professional school…. We [at the AOM] are global. Other countries are looking like us – that is the sad part. We are embedded [in a system] – a business school within a university with different purposes. We are forced to play along with that game. The medical and engineering schools do not have the same pressures. They | – and include the applied and professional parts. This [integration] needs to be reflected in our journals, and in [accepting] published research in books…." |

(Continued)

Name	Impact Factors and Citations	Journal Articles and Rankings	Books and Reports	Better Measures	Faculty Evaluations	Big Problems	Recommendations for AOM
Scholar 8 (continued)					department, Strategy/OT and OB/Micro have 2 lists. The obvious ones are included, ASQ, AMJ, AMR, for example. We consider publications in a small list of elite journals".	are regulated. They do not have university [administrators] telling them what to do. Our stakeholders [on the other hand] can be anyone".	"We need the right peer group to evaluate measures like op-eds and blogs. Currently, we have too few people who can do it, so you have to reach out to experts. Most academic institutions would never set that up. But, outside acceptance
Scholar 9 (USA)		"Some journal articles are very important… Most research [that we publish in academic journals] is hack research with simple-minded problems that have no consequence, done by simple-minded people who	"Books are important".	"There is no perfect measure of impact…For better measures of scholarly impact you need a different type of thinking. I would count op-eds, letters to the editor, blogs, etc. But, if you try to include them, you will get jealousy, condescension, put downs, etc. People will say you are	"For tenure, you have to abide by traditional criteria or you cannot get through the faculty…The Academy does not really value the ability and willingness to communicate to a wider public. To become a public intellectual, you generally have to endure ridicule,	"To want to be a public intellectual, there has to be something in a person's history that marks them out for it. It is part of their character, their DNA. But, academics are so fearful people, so afraid of sticking out and of doing	

Scholar 9 (continued)					
	otherwise would not be employed, talking to similarly simple-minded people".	'not a serious academic'… Consulting is very important… Consulting is applied research. Of course, there is hack consulting, but there is also hack research".	hostility, and jealousy. I would keep working towards becoming a public intellectual if you have the desire, but I'd stay relatively quiet until you get tenure. Otherwise you arouse too much hatred and suspicion. To make it in the Academy you have to do so through the established processes. And, that's what most people will ever do. They will also be hostile to those who communicate to wider publics and write legibly and intelligently. If	something different… Most people do not go through grad school with a mentor who has been both a public intellectual and an internationally accepted scholar. Their role models are very narrow and specialized… Everyone who has broken out has faced difficulties".	is important. Stephen Gould, Henry Mintzberg can do it. They are exceptions. You can find these exceptions at top schools such as HBS. At Oxbridge you have the peer group [and confidence] to engage in fairy tales…One thing the AOM can do is to give an award for these kinds of activities, perhaps for the best op-ed in Management… Perhaps … intellectual shamans and others can serve as a peer group for evaluating different types of writing.

(Continued)

Name	Impact Factors and Citations	Journal Articles and Rankings	Books and Reports	Better Measures	Faculty Evaluations	Big Problems	Recommendations for AOM
Scholar 9 (continued)					you do not follow established models, you will be spit out of the Academy… However, I would make a requirement for academic evaluation that all academic journal articles also have an accompanying 500–700 op-ed [like] essay. This essay would be written for a lay audience where the authors explain why their research matters to managers. If I founded a business school, it would be founded on that principle. Every bit of academic research would		It could be a subgroup of the Academy, even. These people have taken risks and broken out. The [quest for scholarly impact] cannot be carried out by one means alone. It has to be repeated and widespread".

Scholar 9 (continued)				"also have an accompanying op-ed explaining the significance of what the authors have done for a lay audience".	"Our system does not encourage good or useful science. We value expedience: Do what it takes to publish in journals. Tackle problems that are popular with journals and editors. This research does not call attention to social problems… Much of our published research] would not fit the criteria of sound science.	"The Academy [of Management] can do a lot. [Support of this project] shows that the current Board is trying to fight the tradition of the status quo. The Academy has been so successful. Attendance at our annual meetings is the highest among any professional association. So, we have also become a victim of our own success, and there is little
Scholar 10 (USA)	"We tend to know which are the real top journals. These are not based on the Impact Factor. Impact Factor is very artificial – it is artificially constructed from citation patterns. Top journals are more about the importance of ideas".	"A plus journals have decreased in importance for the world. No one in the business world cares about our journals or our research. Even people in the field do not seem to care. Most seem to care about is the appearance of good scholarship… I have a subjective list [of A plus journals] which includes ASQ, AMJ, JAP, and SMJ, etc., all	"Books are important to report a large-scale project or research with multiple studies and samples. Journals take a very incremental approach to research. So much of what we see in these journals is a futile exercise of manipulating raw data with irrelevant ideas".	"Many young scholars receive the advice to follow the requirements and not worry about pursuing true science. They can do that after they receive tenure. However, by the time someone passes tenure it is too late to change their research habit or approach. We need to change the front end, not after 6–10 years of doing research that is neither science nor important. At	"I agree with [Aguinis, Shapiro, et al.] that a well-rounded portfolio approach should be taken for evaluating. Not every piece of research can be published in a top-quality journal. Research published in second-tier journals and B+ journals can also be meaningful… Any evaluation for a tenure promotion should include	

(Continued)

Name	Impact Factors and Citations	Journal Articles and Rankings	Books and Reports	Better Measures	Faculty Evaluations	Big Problems	Recommendations for AOM
Scholar 10 (continued)		of which have rigorously done research. But only 5 percent of the research published in these journals is interesting – the rest is model refinement rather than a better explanation of the phenomena. But, currently 90 percent deals with theory and only 10 percent with phenomena. What happened to the phenomena we were		that point, there is no reason to change…".	an actual reading of the papers and asking the referees to comment on the content and importance of the ideas. To what problems in the social and business world does our research contribute to understanding? What is the importance of the research problem being studied? What is the substantive contribution?"	It does not aim at solving problems important to society and the knowledge has unknown reliability without estimating errors in inference, and the problem of under-determination. Most of our published work in recent years advances the personal preferences of authors or reviewers. When science does not meet the minimum criteria of integrity and	incentive to change. We are now criticized for our lack of relevance – and the Board sees that".

| Scholar 10 (continued) | supposed to be studying?.... We assume that all articles in top journals are of the highest quality; these articles are closer to the truth and have fewer errors. The data show that these assumptions are not correct.... there is not a clear standard of quality or rigor". | epistemic values, it is considered 'junk science'". |

outlets for career-aspiring management academics", with a corresponding under-reliance on ideas, community and society, and excessive "balkanization" as Management scholars became "angels dancing on a pin head" with limited societal impact. Some scholars raised concerns about the universal applicability and acceptance abroad of deficient U.S. faculty-evaluation standards and research approaches that diminish scholarly impact. One scholar categorized the spread of U.S. research standards globally as amounting to "imperialism" and a form of "colonialism", with a lack of regard to context. Major themes follow:

i   ***Journal impact factors as a gauge of influence:*** Despite their widespread use in faculty evaluations, 50 percent of the sample (5 interviewees) indicated that Impact Factors (from publishers such as Clarivate and Scopus) do not indicate scholarly impact, journal quality, or influence, but general acceptance. Indeed, academic and institutional reliance on Impact Factors had led to an overemphasis on narrowly focused and funneled research that may interest other management academics, but not external constituencies. Forty percent of the sample (four interviewees) did not address the issue or respond, and 10 percent of the sample (one interviewee) saw Impact Factors as flawed, but important measures of scholarly impact.

ii   ***Journal articles and rankings:*** Though acknowledging that journal rankings pervade business schools, 70 percent of the sample (7 interviewees) communicated that the higher-ranked the journal, the less likely that the journals' articles would be interesting or applicable to the real world. Thirty percent of the sample (three interviewees) saw journal rankings as playing favorable roles in business schools as they provide avenues to measure stature and to focus debate.

iii   ***Books and consulting/government reports:*** Books, especially monographs, provide greater depth and broader avenues for influence through research; as such, 60 percent of the sample (6 interviewees) favored the inclusion of books in faculty evaluations of research. Thirty percent of the sample (three interviewees) had no response on books, and 10 percent (one interviewee) provided information on how books were incorporated into existing evaluations.

iv   ***Better measures of scholarly impact***: One hundred percent of the sample (ten interviews) agreed that Management needed more complex measures of scholarly impact which included external constituents and practical influence on both business and government policy. However, interestingly, few agreed on what better measures would replace those in existence. Forty percent (four interviewees) specifically mentioned the AOM's project on scholarly impact and the survey of members as a very promising start on building alternative measures to journal rankings and citations.

v **Big problems:** The overarching problems that the interviews identified included: Academic researchers focusing on journal editors' preferences to get published, rather than on impactful and meaningful research (60 percent, 6 interviewees); inability to incorporate non-U.S. knowledge of practice and relations, and not just publishable research, into the stock of Management knowledge (10 percent); need for greater emphasis on teaching effectiveness (10 percent); and differences in Business School's and the rest of the University's purposes and focus (10 percent). The interviewees in Asia and Europe also saw a troubling isomorphism among measures of scholarly impact adopted by local universities and U.S. universities, which they saw as harmful to doing impactful research in their regions, and as ignoring local talent, history, context, and strategic investments.

vi **Faculty evaluations:** Sixty percent (six interviewees) communicated that current evaluation procedures tend to push faculty to publish in a limited number of journals with little attention to influence or true impact. These interviewees also saw a need for true reform in evaluation processes to where senior faculty, administrators, and regulatory institutions nurture and develop, rather than stunt, scholarly impact. Forty percent (four interviewees) indicated that different criteria should have emphases at different stages of academics' careers, with full professors spending significant proportions of their time cultivating external influence.

vii **Recommendations for the AOM:** Recommendations for the AOM ranged from highly specific actions on journals and articles in them (20 percent); to the opportunity for the Board of Governor's to provide strategic direction for the field (60 percent); to broader environmental issues including AACSB accreditation (10 percent).

The ensuing chapter presents an overview of the survey's findings and in-depth exploration of the quantitative analysis we conducted.

Note

1 All semi-structured interviews were conducted by Usha Haley by phone or over Skype; most interviews lasted 45 minutes to an hour. Interviewees were chosen by the Academy of Management's Board of Governors on the basis of their perceived impact on the field of Management including through very high citations, leadership roles in the Academy (e.g., President, Division Head, Academy Fellow), leadership roles in their institutions (e.g., Deans, Provosts), leadership roles as editors of major journals (e.g., *Academy of Management Journal, Strategic Management Journal, Academy of Management Learning & Education*), leadership roles in regulatory bodies (e.g., AACSB, REF), etc.

References

American Association of University Professors (AAUP) (1940) 1940 statement of principles on academic freedom and tenure. https://www.aaup.org/report/1940-statement-principles-academic-freedom-and-tenure

Academy of Management (2018). Strategic plan – Scholarly Impact Report https://aom.org/about-aom/strategic-plan/scholarly-impact-report

Baker, S. E., & Edwards, R. (2012). How many qualitative interviews is enough? Expert voices and early career reflections on sampling and cases in qualitative research. *National Centre for Research Methods Review Paper.* http://eprints.ncrm.ac.uk/2273/4/how_many_interviews.pdf.

Bamberger, P. A. (2018). AMD—Clarifying what we are about and where we are going. *Academy of Management Discoveries, 4*(1), 1–10.

Barad, K. (2007). *Meeting the universe halfway: Quantum physics and the entanglement of matter and meaning.* Durham, NC and London: Duke University Press.

Benney, M., & Hughes, E. C. (1956). Of sociology and the interview: Editorial preface. *American Journal of Sociology, 62*(2), 137–142.

Briggs, C. (1986). *Learning how to ask: A sociolinguistic appraisal of the role of the interview in social science research.* Cambridge: Cambridge University Press.

Court, D., & Abbas, R. (2013). Whose interview is it, anyway? Methodological and ethical challenges of insider–Outsider research, multiple languages, and dual-researcher cooperation. *Qualitative Inquiry, 19*(6), 480–488.

Creswell, J. W. (2007). *Qualitative inquiry & research design: Choosing among five approaches.* Thousand Oaks, CA: Sage.

Deakin, H., & Wakefield, K. (2014). Skype interviewing: Reflections of two PhD researchers. *Qualitative Research, 14*(5), 603–616.

Delbecq, A. L., van de Ven A. H., & Gustafson D. H. (1975). *Group techniques for program planning: A guide to nominal group and Delphi processes.* Palo Alto, CA: Scott Foresman.

Denzin, N. K., & Lincoln, Y. S. (eds.). (2011). *The Sage handbook of qualitative research.* London: Sage Publications.

DeWalt, K. M., & DeWalt, B. R. (2002). *Participant observation: A guide for fieldworkers.* Walnut Creek, CA: AltaMira Press.

Giddens, A. (1990). *The consequences of modernity.* Stanford, CA: Stanford University Press.

Lofland, J., Snow, D. A., Anderson, L., & Lofland, L. H. (2006). *Analyzing social settings: A guide to qualitative observation and analysis* (4th ed.). Belmont, CA: Thomson Wadsworth.

Seidman, I. E. (1991). *Interviewing as qualitative research: A guide for researchers in education and the social sciences.* New York: Teacher's College.

Vagle, M. D. (2018). *Crafting phenomenological research.* New York: Routledge.

Van Manen, M. (2016). *Research lived experience: Human science for an action sensitive pedagogy.* New York: Routledge.

Villa, E. Q. (2017). *Using in-depth interviews as a primary source of data for developing case studies.* London: Sage Publications Ltd.

Ziman, J. M. (2000). *Real science: What it is, and what it means.* New York: Cambridge University Press.

4 Quantitative data, analysis, and results

Usha C. V. Haley and Melanie C. Page

This chapter begins with a discussion on methodology and sampling for a survey of the Academy of Management's (AOM's) membership. We then describe the analysis and highlight key results. Finally, we analyze some of the key results by professorial rank.

4.1 Sampling & methodology

The previous chapter covered our use of thematic analysis to isolate the constructs in our study. We employed surveys to move from the theoretical to the operational, and then to the observed (Saris & Gallhofer, 2007). When constructing our survey on scholarly impact, we paid special attention to measurement validity; we reflected on alternative choices about the wording of questions and response scales for the indicators, and included additional external measures (such as membership breakdowns by region) to ascertain validity and data quality. For delivery mode, we chose online surveys of the AOM's membership because they provided wide and immediate geographical reach; our surveys also could display on mobile platforms. Our delivery mode thereby enabled responses from a large swathe of the AOM's membership and our abilities to make inferences from our sample to a general population of social-science researchers. We employed mostly close-ended questions, with options for more extensive, write-in options (Epstein, 2013). **Appendix 2** includes the survey we administered.

In our probability survey (Neuman, 2012), recruitment occurred from a randomly generated list of the AOM's members, all of whom had chances to participate in the survey through an emailed link. Research has shown that social-desirability bias becomes less prevalent with self-administered surveys rather than interviewer-administered

DOI: 10.4324/9780429298981-4

questionnaires (Fuchs & Funke, 2007; Kreuter et al., 2008). In this AOM scholarly impact study, participants self-administered their surveys.

The survey went through two reviews at the level of the AOM's Board of Governors and had a response rate of 19 percent (700 responses out of 3750 emailed surveys). Despite our best efforts, there was a typo on the scale for Qs. 5 where an ordinal-scale category was repeated twice; three respondents contacted us within a few hours of the survey's distribution to alert us to the problem. We immediately corrected the issue, but not before we received 147 responses. We ran 24 t-tests and χ^2 analyses to examine patterns of responses in the affected category, as well as did comparisons with other questions. We concluded that the small number of statistical differences (about 2 percent) was due to sampling error. Overall, we made no adjustment for experiment-wise error rate, even though we undertook quite a few analyses: this is an exploratory, first study of its kind and not a confirmatory, hypothesis-driven study.

4.2 Breakdown of results

Appendix 3 provides a summary overview of the results from the survey. This section interprets some of the findings. Results follow for *Audiences for Research, Indicators of Scholarly Impact, Influence on Business Practice and Government Policy, Interdisciplinary Research, University Support, Impact Factors and Journal Rankings,* and *Ideal Measures of Scholarly Impact.*

i   Audiences for research: **Table 4.1** presents descriptive statistics on important audiences for academic research. Overall, respondents viewed all the identified audiences as important, with *labor* and *media* on the lower end, and *top management in companies* and other *Management academics* on the high end. On the open-ended question of other important audiences for academic research, many respondents communicated that they saw the list of audiences on the survey as comprehensive and well thought out. A few suggested consulting firms, all business owners, entrepreneurs, funders, international researchers, academics outside management or social sciences, and high-school students.

ii Indicators of scholarly impact: **Table 4.2** presents descriptive statistics on indicators of scholarly impact. Overall, respondents saw

Table 4.1 Important Audiences for Academic Research (Low 1–High 5)

	Mean	Std. Deviation
Top management in cos.	4.26	.948
Middle management in cos.	3.82	.989
Lower management and non-managers in cos.	3.29	1.108
Management academics	4.48	.808
Social Science academics	4.06	.861
Students	4.00	.936
Media	3.53	1.007
Government and policymakers	4.08	.945
Industry assoc.	3.69	.952
NGOs	3.70	.941
Labor	3.41	1.047
Society	3.89	.976
N = 642		

Table 4.2 Indicators of Scholarly Impact (Low 1–High 5)

	Mean	Std. Deviation
Scholarly articles in top-ranked journals	4.49	.812
Scholarly articles in lower-ranked journals	3.26	1.005
Articles in practitioner and industry publications	3.88	.900
Media coverage of research	3.72	.913
Scholarly citations to research	4.21	.888
Search-engine mentions	3.46	1.092
Consulting	3.64	1.008
Invited keynotes	3.78	.917
Conference presentations	3.71	.963
Direct regulatory influence	3.75	.979
Invited public speeches	3.68	.955
Executive teaching	3.70	1.022
Corporate and government board memberships	3.32	1.073
Appearance on course reading lists	3.59	.999
Academic journal editorial boards	3.85	1.028
Op-eds, documentaries, media publications	3.47	.998
Scholarly books	3.94	.863
Practitioner-oriented books	3.72	.954
Textbooks	3.55	1.004
Book chapters	3.54	.958
Competitive research grants	3.93	.940
Article downloads	3.75	1.021
Awards and honors for research	3.82	1.024
Altmetrics	3.34	1.002
N = 582		

all the indicators as above neutral. The lowest indicators were *corporate boards, lower-tiered journal articles,* and *altmetrics. Top-tiered journal articles* had the highest ranking, followed by *scholarly citations.* A repeated measures test (p <.05) between *top-tiered* and *lower-tiered* showed that top-tiered publications were far more important (4.49 vs. 3.26). On the open-ended question of other important indicators, respondents listed actual changes to practice, use of research in practice, dissemination in a variety of outlets, classroom use, and student success. Several expressed frustrations over the reliance on top-tiered journal articles to measure impact as evidenced in these two quotes:

> Any practical impact is important as this is management – not natural sciences. The academic, theoretical discussion currently taking place in the major journals have no impact whatsoever, but nobody dares to admit that. It is like the emperor's new clothes…So my answer is that anything that is beneficial to society, people or organizations should be a measure of impact, rather than being part of the discussion in the major journals. We have been reframing practices, routines, knowledge, etc. for many years, but it has led nowhere.

Similarly, a second respondent wrote: "Do we save lives? Do we help companies not die? Do we save jobs? If so these are the impacts. If not, and I suspect we don't, impact is just citation-based and self-referenced within Academia".

iii   Influence on business practices: **Table 4.3** presents descriptive statistics on whether scholarly impact should include extent of changes on business practices. Respondents saw this indicator as above moderately important with a mean of 3.50 (n = 577). 23.4

Table 4.3 Importance of Influencing Business Practices

	Valid Percent	*Cumulative Percent*
Not at all important	6.6	6.6
Somewhat important	14.7	21.3
Moderately important	23.9	45.2
Strongly important	31.4	76.6
Intensely important	23.4	100.0
Total	100.0	
N = 577		

percent of the respondents saw the effecting of change in business as intensely important for scholarly impact. Only 6.6 percent selected not at all important on this question.

iv   Influence on government policy: **Table 4.4** presents descriptive statistics on whether scholarly impact should include extent of changes on government policy. Respondents saw this indicator as above moderately important with a mean of 3.29 (n = 577). 18.5 percent selected intensely important. Only 9.7 percent selected not at all important on this question.

v   Interdisciplinary research: **Table 4.5** presents descriptive statistics on whether inter-disciplinary research has more impact than single-discipline research. Respondents indicated probably yes with a mean of 3.72 (n = 577). 27.6 percent of the respondents selected definitely yes on this question. Only 3.5 percent selected definitely not.

vi   University support: **Table 4.6** presents descriptive statistics on the avenues for scholarly impact that institutions supported for tenure and promotion. The highest-rated item was by strongly considering *top-tiered journal articles* in tenure and promotion decisions (only 1.7 percent strongly disagreed with this statement, and 58.6

Table 4.4 Importance of Influencing Government Policy

	Valid Percent	Cumulative Percent
Not at all important	9.7	9.7
Somewhat important	15.6	25.3
Moderately important	29.6	54.9
Strongly important	26.5	81.5
Intensely important	18.5	100.0
Total	100.0	
N = 577		

Table 4.5 Impact of Interdisciplinary over Single-Discipline Research

	Valid Percent	Cumulative Percent
Definitely not more impactful	3.5	3.5
Probably not more impactful	7.1	10.6
Might or might not be more impactful	31.4	41.9
Probably more impactful	30.5	72.4
Definitely more impactful	27.6	100.0
Total	100.0	
N = 577		

Table 4.6 University Support for Evaluation, Tenure, and Promotion
Criteria (Low 1– High 5)

	Mean	Std. Deviation
Strongly considers publications in top-tier journals	4.54	.889
Gives monetary rewards for publications in top-tier journals	2.66	1.485
Strongly considers publications in practitioner journals	2.84	1.154
Strongly considers consulting activities	2.32	1.239
Strongly considers media coverage, testimonies, and outreach	2.55	1.091
Strongly considers obtaining research grants	3.64	1.151
Strongly considers scholarly citations to research	3.76	1.129
Strongly considers published books	3.07	1.168
N = 570		

Table 4.7 University Support for Respondents' Scholarly Impact

	Valid Percent	Cumulative Percent
Never	2.5	2.5
Almost never	12.6	15.1
Sometimes	47.0	62.1
Almost every time	27.0	89.1
Every time	10.9	100.0
Total	100.0	
N = 570		

percent strongly agreed) followed by considering *scholarly citations* (4.3 percent strongly disagreed, and 24.3 percent strongly agreed) and *grants* (5.4 percent strongly disagreed, and 20.3 percent strongly agreed). The lowest-rated item was through considering *consulting work* (28.3 percent strongly disagreed, and 4.4 percent strongly agreed) or *media coverage* (17 percent strongly disagreed, and 2.1 percent strongly agreed) as part of tenure or promotion evaluations. Relatively little agreement existed on giving *monetary awards for publishing in top-tiered journals* as support (26.4 percent strongly disagreed, and 13.3 percent strongly agreed). **Table 4.7** identifies how respondents felt about their universities supporting their pursuits of scholarly impact. The mean was 3.31 (n=570), indicating respondents felt sometimes their universities supported their efforts to pursue scholarly impact. A small number of the respondents (2.5 percent) stated their university never supported

Table 4.8 Impact Factors or Journal Lists as Measures of Scholarly Impact

	Valid Percent	Cumulative Percent
Definitely are not measures	8.2	8.2
Probably are not measures	19.8	28.1
Might or might not be measures	31.9	60.0
Probably are measures	33.5	93.5
Definitely are measures	6.5	100.0
Total	100.0	
N = 570		

Table 4.9 Management Research's Influence (Low 1–High 5)

	Mean	Std. Deviation
On government policy	2.54	.900
On management policy and practice in large enterprises in my country	2.84	.975
On management policy and practice in small- and medium-sized enterprises (SMEs) in my country	2.41	.993
On labor-management relations in my country	2.36	.940
On management theorizing	3.91	.974
On future research practice	3.59	1.009
On teaching	3.63	.936
On my students' career decisions	2.64	1.101
N=560		

their efforts; 10.9 percent said their university always supported their efforts.

vii Impact figures and journal rankings: **Table 4.8** presents descriptive statistics on if respondents thought that impact figures and journal rankings captured scholarly impact. Given their pervasiveness in faculty evaluations, the respondents' ambivalence appears striking. The mean was 3.10 (n = 570), just above neutral. 8.2 percent selected definitely not on this question, and 6.5 percent selected definitely yes.

viii Management research's influence: **Table 4.9** presents descriptive statistics on perceptions of the influence of Management research. With means for 5 of the 8 spheres of research influence as under 3 (neutral), most of the respondents saw Management research as only slightly influential and below neutral in regard to *government policy* (mean 2.54), *management practice* (mean 2.84 for large, and 2.41 for small enterprises), *labor* (mean 2.36) and *students' career* *decisions* (mean 2.64). The highest-ranked spheres of influence which respondents saw as somewhat influential and above neutral included *management theorizing* (mean 3.91), *teaching* (mean 3.63), and *future research practice* (3.59).

ix Ideal measures of scholarly impact: For this open-ended question, many answers came down on the side of *using many factors together to gauge scholarly impact* or a pluralistic conception (see Aguinis et al., 2014), rather than a singular focus on top-tiered journal publications. For example, one respondent stated, "A-lists are meaningless"; another suggested, "A combination of publications, citations, speeches, etc. not one single measure, but a measure that acknowledges different types of research output". A secondary theme dealt with lack of impact and influence on business, policy, and practice. As one respondent stated, "At least do no harm".

4.3 Analysis of scholarly impact by rank

The subsequent subsections analyze differences across ranks and by global regions. All significant results in the analysis are at p <.05.

The respondents consisted of 145 assistant professors, 130 associate professors, 163 full or named professors, 19 deans, 5 research professors and 10 practice professors (combined in analyses), 27 adjunct professors, 131 graduate students and post-docs, 53 people in business or government, 17 unemployed, emeritus, and other. If a respondent identified in two categories, we assigned him or her to the category we assumed as the primary role. For example, if a respondent identified as a businessperson and also an adjunct, we assumed she or he was working full time in a business, and teaching a class as an adjunct based on that full-time position. If a respondent identified as dean and full professor, we chose their higher-ranked position of dean. We examined by rank the importance of each avenue for scholarly impact. Our analysis showed career academics' tendencies against more-applied, practice, and teaching-related outputs of scholarly impact as opposed to businesspersons, doctoral students, and administrators.

Our $\chi 2$ analysis indicated as important and significant (p <.05) *industry publications, consulting, executive teaching*, and *practice books*: all showed a similar pattern in that fewer associate and full professors than expected chose the "Very Important" category and more than expected adjunct, research/practice, and business/government respondents chose that category. *Executive teaching* displayed the same pattern, but applied only to associates and business/government respondents. *Practitioner books* also displayed the same pattern, but only for associates and business/government respondents (and to a lesser degree to research/practice and adjuncts).

Similar findings emerged when looking at mean score differences (by a series of one-way ANOVAs, followed by Tukey's Honestly Significant Difference or HSD tests if the overall F value was significant at p <.05): again, differences arose by rank on *industry publications, consulting, executive teaching,* and *practitioner books.* Additional differences arose on *corporate boards, appearance on course lists, op-eds, scholarly books,* and *textbooks.* Tukey's post-hoc analyses tests (p <.05) showed that assistant (3.82), associate (3.71), and full professors (3.73) rated *industry publications* lower than did business/government people (4.34) did. Similarly, assistant (3.56), associate (3.41), and full professors (3.43) rated *consulting* lower than business/government persons (4.12) and adjuncts (4.30) did; and associates and fulls also rated consulting lower than graduate students/post-docs (3.84). Associates (3.43) and fulls (3.54) rated *executive teaching* as less important than business/government persons (4.14). Associates (3.12) rated *presence on corporate boards* lower than adjuncts (3.95). Assistants (3.64), associates (3.51), and fulls (3.61) rated *practitioner books* lower than business/government persons (4.31). Similarly, assistants (3.23), associates (3.45), and fulls (3.56) rated *textbooks* lower than business/government people (4.06).

Initial Tukey's tests for *course lists, scholarly books,* and *op-eds* revealed no significant pairwise differences; consequently, we looked for patterns in the significant mean differences (p <.05) for these tests by Fisher's Least Significant Difference (LSD). As a less-stringent test than Tukey's, more pairwise differences end up significant in Fisher's than Tukey's, which readers should keep in mind when interpreting results. We found that deans (4.0) viewed *course lists* as more important than assistant professors (3.35) and research/practice professors (3.15); full professors (3.6) saw *course lists* as more important than assistant professors. Assistant professors (3.25) rated *op-eds* lower than graduate students/post-docs (3.5). Full professors (4.10), adjuncts (4.3), and business/government people (4.18) rated *scholarly books* higher than assistant professors (3.78). These differences probably indicate the unfavored position of *books, course lists,* and *op-eds* in academic evaluations for tenure.

We found no significant rank differences on importance of *top-tiered journal publications*: all groups rated this avenue as above 4.13 (above 4.4 except for other, unemployed, and emeritus categories; a cap existed at 4.5). Similarly, no group differences emerged for *lower-tiered journal publications*; all groups rated above 2.9 (with a cap at 3.6).

The next chapter discusses differences in perceptions of scholarly impact by geographical region.

References

Aguinis, H., Shapiro, D. L., Antonacopoulou, E. P., & Cummings, T. G. (2014). Scholarly impact: A pluralist conceptualization. *Academy of Management Learning & Education, 13*(4), 623–639.

Epstein, L. (2013). *Get better data and simplify analysis: Qualitative vs. quantitative questions.* Retrieved 10 August 2015, from: www.surveymonkey.com/blog/en/blog/2013/04/10/qualitative-vs-quantitative

Fuchs, M., & Funke, F. (2007). Multimedia Web surveys: Results from a field experiment on the use of audio and video clips in Web surveys. In Trotman, M., Burrell, T., Gerrard, L., Anderton, K., Basi, G., Couper, M., Morris, K., Birks, D., Johnson, A. J., Baker, R., Rigg, M., Taylor, S., & Westlake, A. (eds.), *The challenges of a changing world* (pp. 63–80). Proceedings of the Fifth International Conference of the Association for Survey Computing. Berkeley, CA: ASC.

Kreuter, F., Presser, S., & Tourangeau, R. (2008). Social desirability bias in CATI, IVR, and web surveys: The effects of mode and question sensitivity. *Public Opinion Quarterly, 72*(5), 847–865. https://doi.org/10.1093/poq/nfn063

Neuman, W. L. (2012). *Understanding research.* Boston, MA: Pearson Education, Inc.

Saris, W. E., & Gallhofer, I. N. (2007). *Design, evaluation, and analysis of questionnaires for survey research.* Hoboken, NJ: John Wiley & Sons.

5 Global differences in measuring scholarly impact

Usha C. V. Haley and Melanie C. Page

This chapter explores some of the regional differences and similarities that emerged in measurements of scholarly impact across geographical regions. First, we provide an overview of how institutions use evaluations of scholarly impact around the world. Next, we describe our geographic sample and provide an overview of some results. Finally, we focus on the differences and similarities that emerged across regions in evaluations of scholarly impact.

5.1 Think global, act local

Several countries (including Australia, Belgium, France, Italy, New Zealand, and the United Kingdom) conduct national evaluations that require research to account for funding and to show returns on investment (Abramo & D'Angelo 2011; Derrick & Pavone 2013). These systems evaluate academic institutions' impact not just on scientific progress, but also on the economy, environment, defense, and public health. Since 2014 the United Kingdom, for example, has had the Research Excellence Framework (REF, that replaced the Research Assessment Exercise, RAE) which evaluates universities using peer review, case studies, and various impact metrics that for 2021 evaluations account for 25 percent of the score (Thwaites, 2014; King's College London and Digital Science, 2015; REF 2021). National evaluations of research have internal components to allocate research funds and external components to evaluate national research in global contexts (Bulaitis, 2017). The data showed that increasingly these evaluation systems rely on Impact Factors and journal rankings, demonstrating isomorphism.

National, institutional, and researchers' evaluations around the world appear to rely on similar metrics for scholarly impact.

DOI: 10.4324/9780429298981-5

However, we do not currently have metrics to measure the impact of management research in individual geographical regions: as we described in Chapter 1, research outputs tend to concentrate in a relatively small area – the United States and Europe. If management research outputs follow the same trajectory as in other fields, such as medicine, the United States primarily, followed by Europe, may deliver nearly 60 percent of all research outputs recorded on databases such as Scopus, despite making up less than 20 percent of the global population (Lamanna & Bruijins, 2018). Yet, research has repeatedly shown that results from first-world, developed markets do not translate to third-world emerging markets. As Lamanna and Bruijins (2018) elaborated for medical research, in emerging markets, patients differ, pathogens vary, and infrastructures diverge in their human, physical, and technological resources. Quite literally, lifesaving methods and solutions in Los Angeles may prove lethal in Lusaka (Andrews et al., 2017). In management research, cultural and historical differences further interact with infrastructure, human, physical, and technological differences (Kieser, 1994; Haley et al., 2013). Consequently, regional and geographical contexts assume significance for conversations on scholarly impact (Haley & Haley, 2016).

5.2 Geographic sample and findings

The geographical breakdown for our study consisted of respondents from North America; Europe; Asia; Africa and the Middle East; and Latin America.

i *North America:* The scholarly impact survey had 394 respondents from North America (the United States and Canada). U.S. and Canadian survey respondents took an inclusive view of audiences for their research, viewing every listed audience for academic research as above neutral; additionally, *management academics, top management in companies, social-science academics,* and *government policymakers* were seen as very important audiences for academic research (see **Table 5.1**). U.S. and Canadian respondents also had a pluralistic view of scholarly impact indicators, ranking every indicator as above neutral; however, *articles in top-tier journals, scholarly citations,* and *scholarly books* were seen as very important indicators of scholarly impact (see **Table 5.2**). U.S. and Canadian respondents indicated strong agreement on only one

Table 5.1 Audiences for Academic Research: USA and Canada

	Minimum	*Maximum*	*Mean*	*Std. Deviation*
Top management in cos.	**1**	**5**	**4.22**	**.988**
Middle management in cos.	1	5	3.81	.995
Lower management in cos.	1	5	3.26	1.120
Management academics	**1**	**5**	**4.51**	**.779**
Social Science academics	**1**	**5**	**4.06**	**.854**
Students	1	5	3.98	.971
Media	1	5	3.51	1.001
Govt. policymakers	**1**	**5**	**4.04**	**.965**
Industry associations	1	5	3.64	.974
NGOs	1	5	3.64	.978
Labor	1	5	3.35	1.100
Society	1	5	3.80	1.008

Table 5.2 Indicators of Scholarly Impact: USA and Canada

	Minimum	*Maximum*	*Mean*	*Std. Deviation*
Articles in top-tier journals	**1**	**5**	**4.50**	**.808**
Articles in lower-ranked journals	1	5	3.36	.969
Articles in practitioner publications	1	5	3.95	.861
Media coverage	1	5	3.69	.925
Scholarly citations	**1**	**5**	**4.21**	**.899**
Search-engine mentions	1	5	3.38	1.115
Consulting	1	5	3.61	1.030
Keynotes	1	5	3.71	.907
Academic conference presentations	1	5	3.76	.938
Regulatory influence	1	5	3.80	.988
Invited public speeches	1	5	3.58	.960
Executive teaching	1	5	3.65	1.034
Corporate or govt. boards	1	5	3.28	1.057
Course reading lists	1	5	3.60	1.007
Journal editorial boards	1	5	3.86	1.030
Op-eds	1	5	3.43	1.013
Scholarly books	**1**	**5**	**4.01**	**.837**
Practitioner books	1	5	3.78	.952
Textbooks	1	5	3.50	1.030
Book chapters	1	5	3.57	.970
Competitive research grants	1	5	3.93	.954
Article downloads	1	5	3.81	.986
Awards	1	5	3.88	1.011
Altmetrics	1	5	3.28	1.000

indicator of the university's support of scholarly impact – that of strongly considering *publications in top-tier journals*. Other indicators either got no support or middling support (see **Table 5.3**).

Additionally, the respondents indicated that universities only sometimes supported their own efforts to pursue scholarly impact (mean 3.36 on a scale of 1 minimum to 5 maximum). Presumably, this university support was forthcoming mostly in the respondents' pursuit of journal articles in top-tier publications. The respondents were essentially neutral (mean 3.09 on a scale of 1 minimum to 5 maximum) on Impact Factors and journal rankings as adequate indicators of scholarly impact; yet, data show that universities mostly evaluate their faculty on these figures and rankings.

ii *Europe:* The scholarly impact survey had 193 respondents from Europe (including the European Union, the United Kingdom, and Eastern Europe). **Table 5.4** indicates important audiences for research and major indicators of scholarly impact. Despite national

Table 5.3 University Support for Scholarly Impact: USA and Canada

	Minimum	Maximum	Mean	Std. Deviation
Publications in top-tier journals	**1**	**5**	**4.50**	**.962**
Monetary rewards	1	5	2.29	1.328
Publications in practitioner journals	1	5	2.84	1.159
Consulting	1	5	2.20	1.249
Media coverage	1	5	2.49	1.090
Research grants	1	5	3.39	1.173
Scholarly citations	1	5	3.79	1.066
Books	1	5	3.06	1.218

Table 5.4 Very Important Audiences for Research (A) and Very Important Indicators of Scholarly Impact (I): Europe (Eastern Europe, the EU, & the UK)

	N	Minimum	Maximum	Mean	Std. Deviation
A: Top management in companies	181	1	5	4.22	.927
A: Management academics	**181**	**1**	**5**	**4.40**	**.874**
A: Social Science academics	181	1	5	4.08	.853
A: Students	181	1	5	4.01	.894
A: Govt. policymakers	181	1	5	4.10	.952
I: Articles in top-tier journals	**159**	**1**	**5**	**4.43**	**.853**
I: Scholarly citations	159	1	5	4.09	.937

evaluations exercises such as REF, survey respondents from Europe considered several audiences (A) for scholarly research as highly important (four and above on a five-point scale), and only two indicators of scholarly impact (I) as highly important (four and above on a five-point scale). These respondents indicated *other Management academics* served as the most important audience, and *articles in top-tier journals* provided the most important indicator of scholarly impact.

iii *Asia:* The scholarly impact survey had 55 respondents from Asia. **Table 5.5** indicates that survey respondents from Asia considered several audiences (A) for scholarly research as highly important (four and above on a five-point scale), and several indicators of scholarly impact (I) as highly important (four and above on a five-point scale). These respondents indicated a tie between *other Management academics* and *top management in companies* as the most important audience, and *articles in top-tier journals* as the most important indicator of scholarly impact.

iv *Oceania:* The scholarly impact survey had 29 respondents from Oceania (Australia and New Zealand). As **Table 5.6** shows, survey respondents from Oceania considered several audiences (A) for scholarly research as highly important (four and above on a

Table 5.5 Very Important Audiences for Research (A) and Very Important Indicators of Scholarly Impact (I): Asia

	N	Minimum	Maximum	Mean	Std. Deviation
A: Top management in companies	**50**	**1**	**5**	**4.50**	**.839**
A: Middle management in companies	50	1	5	4.08	1.027
A: Management academics	**50**	**3**	**5**	**4.50**	**.614**
A: Social science academics	50	1	5	4.08	.877
A: Govt. policymakers	50	1	5	4.06	.913
A: Society	50	1	5	4.08	.900
I: Articles in top-tier journals	**47**	**1**	**5**	**4.57**	**.744**
I: Articles in practitioner publications	47	1	5	4.00	.956
I: Scholarly citations	47	3	5	4.36	.673
I: Journal editorial boards	47	1	5	4.11	.866
I: Competitive research grants	47	1	5	4.00	.885

Table 5.6 Very Important Audiences for Research (A) and Very Important Indicators of Scholarly Impact (I): Oceania (Australia and New Zealand)

	N	Minimum	Maximum	Mean	Std. Deviation
A: Top management in companies	25	2	5	4.44	.768
A: Middle management in companies	25	2	5	4.04	.611
A: Management academics	**25**	**4**	**5**	**4.56**	**.507**
A: Social Science academics	25	2	5	4.04	.841
A: Students	25	3	5	4.32	.690
A: Govt. policymakers	25	2	5	4.28	.792
A: Industry associations	25	2	5	4.08	.759
A: Society	25	2	5	4.04	.676
I: Articles in top-tier journals	23	2	5	4.30	.974
I: Scholarly citations	**23**	**2**	**5**	**4.35**	**.775**
I: Scholarly book	23	1	5	4.00	.905
I: Competitive research grants	23	2	5	4.04	.825

five-point scale), and several indicators of scholarly impact (I) as highly important (four and above on a five-point scale). These respondents indicated that *other Management academics* served as the most important audience, and *scholarly citations* provided the most important indicator of scholarly impact.

v   *Africa and Middle East:* The scholarly impact survey had 15 survey respondents from Africa (3) and the Middle East (12) which we combined for the analysis. As **Table 5.7** shows, survey respondents from Africa and the Middle East considered several audiences (A) for scholarly research as highly important (four and above on a five-point scale), and several indicators of scholarly impact (I) as highly important (four and above on a five-point scale). These respondents indicated that *government policymakers* served as the most important audience, and *articles in top-tier journals* provided the most important indicator of scholarly impact.

vi *Latin America:* As Latin America had only 12 combined respondents from different regions, we conducted no quantitative analysis. A qualitative interpretation of the results follows in Chapter 6.

Table 5.7 Very Important Audiences for Research (A) and Very Important
Indicators of Scholarly Impact (I): Africa and the Middle East

	N	Minimum	Maximum	Mean	Std. Deviation
A: Top management in companies	14	3	5	4.43	.852
A: Management academics	14	1	5	4.29	1.437
A: Social science academics	14	1	5	4.14	1.231
A Students	14	2	5	4.14	.864
A: Govt. policymakers	**14**	**3**	**5**	**4.50**	**.650**
A: NGOs	14	3	5	4.07	.475
A: Society	14	3	5	4.43	.756
I: Articles in top-tier journals	**12**	**4**	**5**	**4.83**	**.389**
I: Articles in practitioner publications	12	3	5	4.33	.778
I: Scholarly citations	12	2	5	4.50	.905
I: Consulting	12	3	5	4.17	.937
I: Keynotes	12	1	5	4.00	1.206
I: Academic conference presentations	12	3	5	4.25	.754
I: Executive teaching	12	2	5	4.00	.953
I: Course reading lists	12	2	5	4.08	.900
I: Scholarly books	12	4	5	4.67	.492
I: Practitioner books	12	3	5	4.25	.754
I: Textbooks	12	3	5	4.33	.651
I: Book chapters	12	3	5	4.08	.669
I: Competitive research grants	12	2	5	4.25	.965
I: Article downloads	12	2	5	4.25	.866
I: Awards	12	1	5	4.00	1.206

5.3 Analysis of geographical differences

Because of the limited number of respondents in some geographical sectors, we could only do statistical analysis on a few indicators. Analysis follows discussing isomorphism of evaluation standards, indicators of scholarly impact, Impact Factors and journal rankings, influence of management research, and universities' support of scholarly impact pursuits.

i *Isomorphism*: Several similarities in measuring scholarly impact existed across the geographical regions, reinforcing the isomorphism that the qualitative data and personal interviews had indicated was happening globally. These similarities may indicate a drive for legitimacy in the global marketplace for research and students (see Deephouse, 1996). Frumkin and Galaskiewicz (2004) argued that public-sector institutions (such as, in our case, universities) and mechanisms (such as, in our case, national evaluations of scholarly output) do not just serve as catalysts of similarities – but also as objects of mimetic, normative, and coercive pressures. Statistical tests revealed no differences across region on the importance of any of the *audiences* for scholarly research. Similarly, no significant differences emerged across global regions on the importance of changing *business practices* or *government policy* for scholarly impact. No significant regional differences emerged on the importance of *interdisciplinary research* or in feelings that *universities offer scant support to respondents in their individual pursuits of scholarly activity with impact.*

ii *Indicators of Scholarly Impact:* Significant regional differences emerged on some indicators of scholarly impact (p <.05) that we explored further with Tukey's Honestly Significant Difference (HSD) test. Regional differences emerged on the importance of *lower-ranked journals, industry publications, invited keynotes, invited public speeches,* and *book chapters.* For all analyses, lower scores reflect less importance. For *lower-ranking journals,* Europe scored lower than North America (3.04 vs. 3.36); for *industry publications,* Europe scored lower than North America (3.69 vs. 3.95); for *invited public talks,* Europe (3.95) scored higher than North America (3.58) and Latin America (2.92); and for *invited keynote talks,* Europe scored higher than Latin America (3.94 vs. 3.17). Thus, Europeans appear to put less importance on *lower-tiered journals* and *industry publications,* but higher importance on *invited talks* than did North America and/or respondents from Latin America. For *book chapters,* the Tukey's HSD comparisons showed no significant regional differences; thus, we looked at this variable using Fisher's Least Significant Difference (LSD) analyses, and found that Europeans (3.37) were lower than Latin America (4), Africa/ME (4.08), and North America (3.57).

iii *Impact Factors and Journal Rankings:* On the question regarding *Impact Factors* and *journal rankings* as reflecting scholarly impact, North Americans (3.09) and Europeans (2.94) scored significantly lower (p <.05) than Asians (3.68) by Tukey's HSD tests. Low scores reflect views that rankings do not reflect scholarly impact.

iv *Influence of Management Research:* On questions regarding how *influential management research has been with various stakeholders,* we found that by Fisher's LSD tests (p <.05), for *influencing government policy,* Europe scored lower than Africa (2.55 vs. 3.08) and North America scored lower than Asia (2.46 vs. 2.76), where low scores reflect less influence.

v   *University Support for Scholarly Impact:* Statistical tests revealed that respondents' evaluations of their universities' support in pursuing scholarly impact varied significantly (p <.05) by region on *monetary rewards.* North America (2.29) was seen as less likely to give *monetary rewards* than Latin America (3.67); Europe (2.92) was less likely to give *monetary rewards* than North America and Asia (3.64); North America scored lower than Asia; and Oceania (3.43) was less likely to give *monetary rewards* than Latin America. On the question of considering *consulting* in promotion or tenure decisions, we found that North America (2.20) was less likely (p <.05) to consider consulting than Asia (2.77). Finally, on the question of considering *research grants* in promotion or tenure decisions (p <.05), Africa (3.42) and Asia (3.45) were less likely to consider grants than Oceania (4.57); Europe (4.06) was more likely to consider *research grants* than Asia or North America (3.39).

Overwhelmingly, regions across the world identified *other Management academics* as the important audience for research, and *articles in top-tier journals* as the most important indicator of scholarly impact. Yet, statistical theories of journal review processes show that though articles in top-tier journals receive more citations than those in lower-tier journals, about half the articles published are not among the best ones submitted to those journals; indeed, some of the articles that belong in the top-tier journals may elicit rejections from up to 5 journals (Starbuck, 2005). Consequently, focusing on top-tier journals may impede development of globally impactful knowledge when mediocre research receives high visibility. For more information on the analyses for these regions and others, please contact the authors.

References

Abramo, G., & D'Angelo, C. (2011). Evaluating research: From informed peer review to bibliometrics. *Scientometrics, 87*(3), 499–514. doi:10.1007/s11192-011-0352-7.

Andrews, B., Semler, M. W., Muchemwa, L., Kelly, P., Lakhi, S., Heimburger, D. C., Mabula, C., Bwalya, M., & Bernard, G. R. (2017). Effect of an early resuscitation protocol on in-hospital mortality among adults with sepsis and hypotension: A randomized clinical trial. *Journal of the American Medical Association, 318*(13), 1233–1240.

Bulaitis, Z. (2017). Measuring impact in the humanities: Learning from accountability and economics in a contemporary history of cultural value. *Palgrave Communications, 3*(1), 1–11.

Deephouse, D. L. (1996). Does isomorphism legitimate?. *Academy of Management Journal, 39*(4), 1024–1039.

Derrick, G. E., & Pavone, V. (2013). Democratizing research evaluation: Achieving greater public engagement with bibliometrics-informed peer review. *Science and Public Policy, 40*(5), 563–575. doi:10.1093/scipol/sct007.

Frumkin, P., & Galaskiewicz, J. (2004). Institutional isomorphism and public sector organizations. *Journal of Public Administration Research and Theory, 14*(3), 283–307.

Haley, G. T., Tan, C. T., & Haley, U. C. V. (2013). *New Asian emperors: The overseas Chinese, their strategies and competitive advantages.* London: Routledge.

Haley, U. C. V., & Haley, G. T. (2016). Think local, act global: A call to recognize competing, cultural scripts. *Management and Organization Review, 12*(1), 205–216.

Kieser, A. (1994). Why organization theory needs historical analyses – And how this should be performed. *Organization Science, 5*, 608–620.

King's College London and Digital Science. (2015). *The nature, scale and beneficiaries of research impact: An initial analysis of Research Excellence Framework (REF) 2014 impact case studies.* London: King's College London.

Lamanna, C., & Bruijns, S. (2018). Measuring regional impact: The case for bigger data. *Learned Publishing, 31*(4), 413–416.

REF (2021), Research Excellence Framework guidance. https://www.ref.ac.uk/guidance/

Starbuck, W. H. (2005). How much better are the most-prestigious journals? The statistics of academic publication. *Organization Science, 16*(2):180–200.

Thwaites, T. (2014). Research metrics: Calling science to account. *Nature, 511*(7510), S57–S60. doi:10.1038/511S57a.

6 Focus on Latin America

José Luis Rivas

In this chapter, we follow up on chapter 5's global differences in scholarly impact by focusing on impact in Latin America. Respondents to the Academy of Management's (AOM's) survey on scholarly impact from Central America (one respondent), South America (ten respondents), and the Caribbean (one respondent) were pooled into Latin America (n=12) for analysis. Because of the cultural and institutional heterogeneity across the region, a qualitative analysis and contextual interpretation yielded more insights for this important market than quantitative analysis.

6.1 Context

The study of Latin America has typically been the purview of political scientists and historians, and management and international-business academics have largely ignored its rich competitive landscape (Cuervo-Cazurra, 2010). Consequently, Bruton et al. (2009) argued that academic and business understandings of Latin America are limited.

After Southeast Asia, Latin America is the second most important emerging region globally with aggregated gross domestic product similar to China's and thrice that of India's (World Bank, 2008). The region represents 14 percent of the world's land mass, but only 8 percent of the world's population (Nicholls-Nixon et al., 2011). Research on national cultures has consistently found that Latin American countries tend to form clusters on various socio-economic indicators (Schwartz, 2007; Inglehart & Carballo, 2008).

The region has high levels of corruption and informal business activities as well as high levels of macroeconomic volatility. It offers an abundance of natural resources as well as low levels of qualified labor. Latin America has long been a world leader in socioeconomic

DOI: 10.4324/9780429298981-6

inequality which has reinforced hierarchies and thwarted efforts to promote education and investment in human capital (Schneider, 2009). Firms in this region additionally tend to follow comparative advantages that emerge from access to natural resources (Vassolo et al., 2011).

Latin America is an important player in the emerging world where economies tend to have inadequate regulatory and enforcement regimes (Bruton et al., 2009). Firms in these countries often pursue fewer formal mechanisms, relying instead on personal relationships and private security arrangements to ensure that parties fulfill contracts (Tung, 2002).

Latin America tends to be connected to key families that dominate local markets and industry bases (Bruton et al., 2009). Educational levels in Latin America remain lower than those in developed countries and East Asia (Schneider, 2009). Due to the importance of family ownership in the region, elites and extended families emerge as primary stakeholders for firms when compared to other institutional systems with wider stakeholder bases (Henisz, 2014). Reliance on close family-related managers as opposed to professional management is also more common than in the Organisation for Economic Co-operation and Development (OECD) countries (Fainshmidt et al., 2018). Compared to other regions, Latin America has a high proportion of working-age people, the usual target for master's and executive education programs. Demographics and the economic liberalization of the early 1990s that brought an array of multinationals into the region created a high demand for management education which in turn fueled an impressive growth of education providers specially focused on MBAs and executive education. The number of schools offering business degrees in Latin America is approximately 2,000, representing 12 percent of business schools worldwide (Alvarado et al., 2018). More open economies and globalization also sparked the internationalization of business schools that started to hire international faculty.

6.2 Differences with other geographic regions

In Latin America,

i Research grants are regarded as "very important" instead of "important". Probably due to the low level of resources that governments invest in science and to the lack of partnerships among businesses, universities, and NGOs.

ii   Board memberships were cited as "important", whereas in other regions they were not mentioned and/or were of less importance. Most business schools in the region are not well connected to local industries and do not use their alumni networks as conduits for achieving more significant bonds. Consequently, boards form important conduits of influence.

iii Capacity to influence business practice has more importance. Probably due to a long history of being practitioner based, most business schools recognize the importance of being "research informed" but aspire to have a more "hands-on" research agenda.

iv   Capacity to influence government policy is more important, probably due to the emerging-market context. Even with the economic liberalization of the early 1990s, institutions are weak and there are "regressions" whenever the political tides turn left.

v   Monetary rewards are more important.

vi   Practitioner journals are more important.

vii Journal lists are perceived as significant by a higher number of respondents (58 vs. 38 percent).

viii Influence of management research on teaching is ranked as important by more respondents (75 vs. 42 percent).

6.3 Implications

The globalization process that Latin America experienced since the early 1990s was also accompanied by an appetite for international accreditations; in 2016 there were 36 Latin American schools from 11 countries with at least one international accreditation (Alvarado et al., 2018).

Having a large sector of the population in the prime working-age range has also engendered more attention on entrepreneurial careers. Youth in the region increasingly aspire for independence but there is also an important sector that aspires to professionalize their family businesses which, as mentioned earlier, constitute key players in the regional business environments.

Latin America has two broad types of business schools. One is practitioner based where most full-time faculty are former consultants/practitioners who aside from teaching will do consulting and writing of business cases. The second is research based where most faculty have PhDs and are mostly focused on research and teaching. The second type of business school is growing in importance but faces serious obstacles. Globalization and the dominance of the American management-education model in Latin America has influenced the shift from practitioner to research-oriented universities but macroeconomic volatility, non-competitive salaries as well as increasing violence has inhibited the attraction of international academics.

Below we present several possibilities that business schools in the region could consider according to the report results cited previously:

i *Research Grants:* Business schools could devote more time to build partnerships with R&D centers, government, and NGOs. Several potential research opportunities exist (i.e., big data, corporate governance) where most stakeholders of this alliance can benefit.

ii *Board Memberships:* Few academics in the region serve on boards. This situation could relate to the predominance of family businesses and lack of culture/tradition of having academics as high-level advisers. More attention could be devoted to building alumni networks and diversifying executive-education programs. Motivated alumni can also provide business schools with research funds related to specific industries or projects.

iii *Capacity to Influence Government Policy:* If business schools emphasized the importance of partnering with local governments, NGOs, and alumni to influence/inform policymakers, the economic liberalization that began in the 1990s could both be accelerated and improved.

iv *Practitioner Journals:* Business schools could incentivize both academic and practitioner journals publications to capture the attention of business leaders and to improve their networking capability.

References

Alvarado, G., Thomas, H., Thomas, L., & Wilson, A. (2018). *Latin America: Management education's growth and future pathways.* Bingley, UK: Emerald Publishing Limited.

Bruton, G. D., Ahlstrom, D., & Puky, T. (2009). Institutional differences and the development of entrepreneurial ventures: A comparison of the venture capital industries in Latin America and Asia. *Journal of International Business Studies, 40*(5), 762–778.

Cazurra, Á. C. (2010). Multilatinas (Latin American Multinationals). *Universia Business Review, 25*(1), 14–33. (written in Spanish)

Fainshmidt, S., Judge, W. Q., Aguilera, R. V., & Smith, A. (2018). Varieties of institutional systems: A contextual taxonomy of understudied countries. *Journal of World Business, 53*(3), 307–322.

Henisz, W. J. (2014). *Corporate diplomacy: Building reputations and relationships with external stakeholders.* Austin, TX: Greenleaf Publishing.

Inglehart, R., & Carballo, M. (2008). Does Latin America exist? A global analysis of cross-cultural differences. *Perfiles Latinoamericanos, 16*(31), 13–38.

Nicholls-Nixon, C. L., Castilla, J. A. D., Garcia, J. S., & Pesquera, M. R. (2011). Latin America management research: Review, synthesis, and extension. *Journal of Management, 37*(4), 1178–1227.

Schneider, B. R. (2009). Hierarchical market economies and varieties of capitalism in Latin America. *Journal of Latin American Studies, 41*(03), 553–575.

Schwartz, S. H. (2007). Value orientations: Measurement, antecedents and consequences across nations. In by Jowell, R., Roberts, C., Fitzgerald, R., & Eva, G. (eds.), *Measuring attitudes cross-nationally: Lessons from the European Social Survey,* 161–193 https://www.iser.essex.ac.uk/research/publications/512128

Tung, R. L. (2008). The cross-cultural research imperative: The need to balance cross-national and intra-national diversity. *Journal of International Business Studies, 39*(1), 41–46.

Vassolo, R. S., De Castro, J. O., & Gomez-Mejia, L. R. (2011). Managing in Latin America: Common issues and a research agenda. *Academy of Management Perspectives, 25*(4), 22–36.

World Bank (2008). *World development report.* Washington, DC: World Bank Group.

7 Implications and suggestions for measuring scholarly impact

Usha C. V. Haley

This final chapter explores and provides some evidence for the Management discipline's effects on external constituents and recommendations for ways forward. The first section discusses the current state of influencing government policy through research. The ensuing sections cover outreach to the media and external constituents' interests in Management research. Next, a quantitative analysis examines some variables affecting reliance on Impact Factors and journal rankings. Finally, the book presents recommendations from impactful Management scholars on ways forward as a discipline.

7.1 Influence on government policy

As we discussed in previous chapters, the Academy of Management's (AOM's) membership viewed scholarly impact as including the extent to which a scholar's work has affected or changed government policy. About 46 percent of the AOM's members considered impact on government policy as either strongly important (27 percent) or intensely important (19 percent); only 10 percent of the members viewed impact on government policy as not at all important as a component of scholarly impact.

Despite the membership's views, and consistent exhortations from the AOM's leadership, (see Hambrick, 1994), the major academic journals in Management appeared to have published very few articles with measurable regulatory impact in the United States. From 1996 to 2020, the AOM and Strategic Management Society's journals garnered:

- One mention in the Environmental Protection Agency Standards of Performance for Greenhouse Emissions, 2014 (of research in the *Academy of Management Review*, 1984);

DOI: 10.4324/9780429298981-7

- One mention in the Department of Labor Office of Disability Employment Policy, 2006 (of research in the *Academy of Management Review*, 1991);
- One mention in the Federal Register, Petition for Waiver of the Terms of the Order Limiting Scheduled Operations at LaGuardia Airport, 2011 (of research in the *Strategic Management Journal*, 1999).

Unfortunately, scarce data prevented assessing regulatory influence in other countries.

Zardo et al. (2018) concluded that two types of interventions affected researchers' abilities to affect governmental policy; both related to policymakers' access to academic research. Zardo et al. (2018) provided evidence that researchers' communication strategies and efforts to build policymakers' skills to access research evidence proved most effective. Yet, despite needs for outreach, more than half of all research that could potentially inform policy lies behind paywalls (Piwowar et al., 2018). Consequently, the 2021 UK Research Excellence Framework (REF, 2021) will only include open-access research: University's performance in the United Kingdom will derive from research that practitioners, policymakers and communities can access

7.2 Outreach through the media

The AOM's membership viewed the media as an important audience for academic research (3.53 on a scale of 1 low to 5 high) and media coverage of research as an important indicator of scholarly impact (3.72 on a scale of 1 low to 5 high). Indeed, major journals' editors, universities and funding agencies are increasingly urging researchers to communicate their findings to the general public. Despite broad consensus about imperatives to communicate to and through media, researchers have continued to categorize these communications as time consuming and limited their own public outreach (Kassab, 2019). Most evaluation metrics still fail to include public outreach as relevant for academics' career advancement, further dampening engagement. Yet, public outreach can benefit academic research, just as academic research can inform public policy and communities. For example, Kassab (2019) conducted a series of statistical analyses drawing on data from a sustainability-science research center in Switzerland. The study concluded that research performance has a positive association

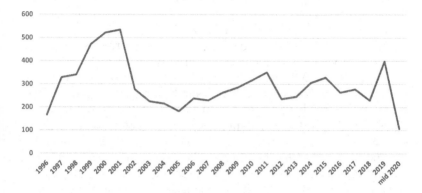

Figure 7.1 Worldwide Media Mentions of Management Journals, 1996–
   mid-2020

Source: Factiva; Journals covered – *Academy of Management Journal, Academy of Management Review, Academy of Management Perspectives/Academy of Management Executive, Academy of Management Learning & Education, and Academy of Management Discoveries.*

with public outreach, with implications for academic incentives and evaluations.

Figure 7.1 charts media mentions of the AOM's major journals (*Academy of Management Journal, Academy of Management Review, Academy of Management Perspectives/Academy of Management Executive, Academy of Management Learning & Education*, and *Academy of Management Discoveries*) from 1990 to June 2020. Media mentions peaked in 2000–2001, but have since fallen, despite an increase in the number of journals and publicly espoused editorial goals for external impact. Mechanical analyses (Leximancer) indicated that key topics in the media mentions focused on compensation policies, attribution theory, compensation adjustments, technical rationality, industry characteristics, physician motivation, salesperson motivation, emotional reactions, and empirical investigations. Most of the topics had a Eurocentric or North American focus.

7.3 Interest from external constituencies

This section provides some exploratory data on external interest in research published in the major academic journals in Management. In 2020, Google had the largest search-market share in the world accounting for 88 percent of global searches (*Statista*, October 2020).

Other scholars (e.g., Aguinis et al., 2012) have used indexing in Google to gauge researchers' scholarly impact. For this research, Google provided normalized data of daily, worldwide searches from 2004 to mid-year 2021, for five of the highest-ranked journals in Management, all of which have included editorial opinions on encouraging impactful research with reach beyond the Academy (e.g., *Academy of Management Perspectives*, 2021). Numbers represent search interest relative to the highest point on the chart (100) by geography and dates. Google divided each data point by total searches in their geographies and the dates they represent to compare relative popularity. Google then scaled the resulting numbers on a range of 0–100 based on the journals' proportions to all searches on all topics. A value of 100 represents peak popularity for a journal; a value of 50 means that a journal is half as popular; a value of 0 means enough data did not exist for a journal.

Corresponding to the research on journal databases such as on the Web of Science (WOS) (covered in chapter 1), Google data revealed that the greatest number of searches for the five Management journals occurred in developed markets (the United States, Canada, the United Kingdom, Germany, Netherlands, and Australia); strong but diminished interest also occurred in some developing or emerging markets (Brazil, India, China, Taiwan, and Pakistan). The great bulk of the world registered insufficient numbers of searches for comparison. These data suggest that the topics covered in the top Management journals may have scant relevance for most external constituencies around the world. As **Figure 7.2** shows, these journals reached their peak popularities in 2004–2005, with the *Academy of Management Journal* and the *Strategic Management Journal* as the most popular journals in Management, attracting the highest search interest from external constituencies during those years. In 2021, normalized data reveal that both these journals enjoy less than 10 percent of the popularity that they had in 2004–2005.

These search data also lag the media mentions covered in **Figure 7.1**, suggesting that media mentions may stoke greater public interest in scholarly research. Indeed, Grant et al. (2018) used mixed-methods, through questionnaires and focus groups, to measure the impact of health-related research broadcasts in two prime-time television programs in the United Kingdom. Follow-up research conducted after the broadcasts showed that participants had enhanced their understandings of the issues, with several revealing that they had changed their behaviors as a result of the research coverage.

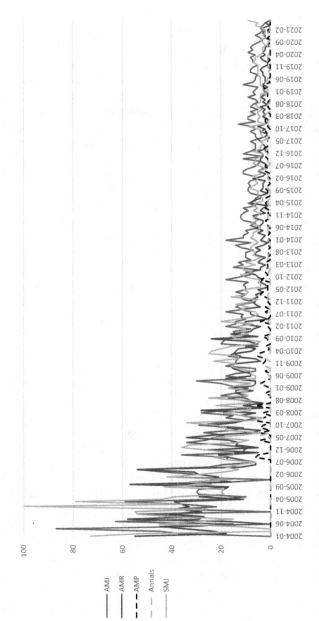

Figure 7.2 Google Normalized Searches for Top Academic Journals in Management, 2004–2021
Source: Google; *Academy of Management Journal (AMJ), Academy of Management Review (AMR), Academy of Management Perspectives (AMP), Academy of Management Annals (Annals), Strategic Management Journal (SMJ).*

7.4 Regression analysis

The author conducted exploratory multinomial logistic regression analysis (GENLIN) to understand support for journal rankings and the Impact Factor in the face of so much contradictory evidence and discussion. Predictor variables included *Audiences for research, Important indicators of scholarly impact, Importance of interdisciplinary research, University support of scholarly impact,* and the *Influence of management research.* With a sample of 700 AOM members, the exploratory model was significant at the .000 level and explained 64 percent of the variance (Nagelkerke, Pseudo R^2). The dependent variable focused on whether *Journal rankings or journal lists (e.g., Journal Impact Figures in Clarivate's Journal Citation Reports or the Financial Times 50 journal-quality list) reflected scholarly impact* (5-point ordinal scale with a low to high range of "definitely not" to "definitely yes"). At 95 percent Wald Confidence Intervals, the final model predicts the dependent variable over and above the intercept-only model, $\chi^2 = 520.8$, p <.000. Some significant results follow:

i   *Audiences for Academic Research*: Respondents that marked journal lists and Impact Figures as **definitely not** reflecting scholarly impact were also more likely (than those who marked these lists and Impact Figures as definitely reflecting scholarly impact) to view *Other academics in the Social Sciences* (p <.05) and *NGOs* (p <.00) as more important audiences for management research; and *Other academics in Management* (p <.05), and *Students* (p <.00) as very unimportant audiences for academic research, with *Industry Associations* as more unimportant (p <.05).

ii   *Indicators of Scholarly Impact*: Respondents that marked journal lists and Impact Figures as **definitely not** reflecting scholarly impact were also more likely (than those who marked these lists and Impact Figures as definitely reflecting scholarly impact) to view *Academic conferences* (p <.05), and *Practitioner-oriented books* (p <.05) as much more important and *Lower-ranked journals* as very important (p <.01) indicators of scholarly impact. These respondents also viewed scholarly articles in *Top-tier journals* as either not important or neutral indicators of scholarly impact (p <.00), *Scholarly citations to academic research* (e.g., WoS, Google Scholar) as not important or very unimportant (p <.00), *Media coverage of research expertise* as more unimportant (p <.02), and *Invited keynote talks* as more unimportant (p <.05).

iii   *Interdisciplinary Research*: Respondents that marked journal lists and Impact Figures as **definitely not** reflecting scholarly impact were also more likely (than those who marked these lists and Impact Figures as definitely reflecting scholarly impact) to view *Interdisciplinary research* as not at all important (p <.00).

iv *University Support of Scholarly Impact*: Respondents that marked journal lists and Impact Figures as **definitely not** reflecting scholarly impact were also more likely (than those who marked these lists and Impact Figures as definitely reflecting scholarly impact) to view *Universities as strongly considering publications in top-tier journals in tenure, promotion, and evaluation decisions* (p <.00) and never or almost never supporting their *Individual pursuits of scholarly impact* (p <.00).

v *Greatest Influence of Management Research:* Respondents that marked journal lists and Impact Figures as **definitely not** reflecting scholarly impact were also more likely (than those who marked these lists and Impact Figures as definitely reflecting scholarly impact) to view Management research as somewhat influential on *Management theorizing* (p <.05), and not at all influential on either *Future research practice* (p <.000) or on *Teaching* (p <.05).

This exploratory research did not control for demographics or region. Yet, we can say with some certainty that respondents who saw journal rankings and Impact Figures as definitely not reflecting scholarly impact (about 20 percent of the sample) also were more likely than respondents who saw these rankings and Impact Figures as definitely reflecting scholarly impact (the reference category, about 7 percent of the sample) to view universities as primarily relying on these scores for evaluations, and as not supporting their individual pursuits of scholarly impact. These members were also more likely to take a broader view of potential audiences and indicators for research, including other social scientists, more likely to value interdisciplinary research, and more likely to view practitioner books, publications in lower-ranked journals, and academic conferences as important. They also were more likely to view Management research as having limited external impact through influencing management theorizing to some extent, but influencing neither future research practice nor teaching.

7.5 Quo Vadis, Management?

This book ends with qualitative observations on the pursuit of impact, as well as recommendations for a more impactful management discipline, and more fulfilled base of management scholars that emerged from interviews with prominent scholars (highlighted in chapter 3); the memberships' open-ended comments on the AOM's survey, and the logistic-regression analysis, buttressed many of the scholars' observations.

Overall, to measure and to achieve scholarly impact, scholars' recommendations reinforced a need to develop composite measures of scholarly impact, to reduce the excessive focus of the field on methodologies and techniques, to increase institutional value on developing ideas important to external constituencies, and to introduce more applications of theories to practice. As one scholar stated:

> The Academy [of Management] can do a lot. [Support of this project] shows that the current Board is trying to fight the tradition of the *status quo*. The Academy has been so successful. Attendance at our annual meetings is the highest among any professional association. So, we have also become a victim of our own success, and there is little incentive to change. We are now criticized for our lack of relevance – and the Board sees that.

Specific themes to measure and to increase scholarly impact follow:

i   *Broaden Measures of Scholarly Impact:* Many lauded the AOM's efforts to broaden awareness of scholarly impact measures. As one scholar stated,

> The AOM should continue to do what it seems to be doing with this project. It sounds like it is trying to broaden the meaning of impact beyond pure citations and provide mechanisms for support of other activities... Through this project the AOM shows that it is aware of concerns and issues and is ready to examine them.

Some indicated aligning scholarly impact figures with the field's mission: "I see this project as very encouraging. We need to look at our mission – and include the applied and professional parts. This [integration] needs to be reflected in our journals, and in [accepting] published research in books..." Others brought up publishers' practices and calculations that shape impact figures.

> Maybe AOM, could do something about publications and calculating impact factors. There is something obviously not going well in publishing. Once an article is published, one cannot do anything more with it, cannot distribute it freely, cannot use the data. The profit motives of the publishing industry

have affected our profession and prevent us from participating freely in the scholar conversation.

ii *Broaden Participation, but Reduce Balkanization:* Several brought up the need to increase broad participation of ideas. As one scholar stated,

> I would advise that we widen our zone of participation outside technical specialists in academic fields to people actually on the firing line. Our ideas take years to come to fruition, but if you do not participate with real people it is useless. You need partnering relationships...We have a schizophrenic system that has failed... Students leave here trying to fit into narrow little blocks to get a job. The practice is rooted in the Academy of Management placement system.

Others stated,

> The areas of interest at SMS [Strategic Management Society] and AOM are also becoming narrower and narrower. We have balkanized interest groups... [we have become] like angels dancing on a pin head. Look at all the OB [Organizational Behavior] and IO [Industrial Organization] interest groups. This balkanization serves as a barrier to scholarship. The impact of our research is on a very narrow segment. My recommendation to the AOM is let us not get too balkanized. There are too many Interest Groups. The AOM is too bloody large. It's like a pharma convention. It has become a meat market for younger people to sell their wares to potential employers.

iii *Increase Assessment Weights for Practical Impact in Journals:* Several scholars argued for shifting the AOM major journals' charge to increase the weight given to practical impact when assessing scholarly contributions. An unnatural "schizophrenia" appeared to characterize journal publications, with some dealing exclusively with methodology, and others exclusively on broader impact. One scholar stated,

> It would be wonderful if AOM changed the focus of their journals to encourage people to do more meaningful research that could make a real contribution to practice and policy in business and government, and avoid the trap of being an incestuous outlet for career-aspiring management academics... In my opinion, *AMJ* [*Academy of Management Journal*] needs

to refocus its energies and judge articles not only on their scholarly contribution and methodology, but on the impact it makes to policy and practice. It is orientated too much to other aspiring, tenure-seeking academics rather than its impact in the real world of policy and practice. Being able to analyze data via the most sophisticated statistical techniques should not be the primary objective of any journal; it should be what contribution it makes to business, society and policy.

The scholars made several specific recommendations on journals, including:

- "I would like to see AOM journals require a major section of an article on implications for government and business policy and practice".
- AOM journals should ask: "To what problems in the social and business world does our research contribute to understanding? What is the importance of the research problem being studied? What is the substantive [rather than methodological] contribution?"
- "I would make a requirement for academic evaluation that all academic journal articles also have an accompanying 500–700 op-ed [like] essay. This essay would be written for a lay audience where the authors explain why their research matters to managers".

iv *Invest in Translating Research for Dissemination:* Some scholars argued for the AOM's investment in developing more innovative and institutionalized ways of translating research for further dissemination by the business press or popular media. As one scholar noted,

Our research world remains relatively insulated. We need to take a far more active approach to closing the gap between research and practice. It cannot be up to the individual researcher to do so. This seems like an important function the Academy of Management might take on.

The scholar made some specific recommendations on dissemination:

The AOM needs to think about creating a portal to have an impact on teaching and practice, to reach managers... We are taking small steps – *AMJ* has developed a website in which researchers talk about their work, and the new *Discoveries* [*Academy of Management Discoveries*] journal is using multimedia to bring their papers to life. The model might be the 'white papers' that you see on the websites of some consulting firms.

v *Initiate Consortia with other Academies:* Some scholars identified overarching agencies, such as AACSB, as unfavorably influencing measures of scholarly impact through artificial journal rankings. They advocated for other business-related consortia to shift ways in which business schools collectively, and not just management academics, evaluate business scholars' impact. As some scholars argued:

> The weight of routines and material practices at the university level is significant. The Academy of Management could have an effect on how impact is defined, perhaps showing how concepts of impact can expand beyond those routines (citations, impact factors, and numbers of articles). We need to act collectively with other academic organizations in Marketing, Finance, Operations, Accounting, and others, if this is our goal, however. Something more systemic is likely required.

Another scholar remarked,

> One gets tenure and promotion with high citations, relatively good teaching, and no impact on the management profession. Some people leap across and actually have some impact. But, we have no incentives as deans to encourage these people... Questions we should ask [for promotion and tenure] are: What have you done that is an interesting area of research? Where do you see this going? How do you develop as a career academic? But, we have an isomorphism of accreditation agencies which reinforce and mandate the P&T system.

vi *Build Impact-Evaluation Groups:* As one scholar stated, "The [quest for scholarly impact] cannot be carried out by one means alone. It has to be repeated and widespread". Specific measures may include forming overarching groups that can evaluate broader impact and honoring academics who pursue other avenues than the *status quo*. Specifically, as one scholar stated:

> We need the right peer group to evaluate measures like op-eds and blogs. Currently, we have too few people who can do it, so you have to reach out to experts. Most academic institutions would never set that up. But, outside acceptance is important. Stephen Gould, Henry Mintzberg can do it. They are exceptions. You can find these exceptions at top schools such as

> HBS... with the peer group [and confidence] to engage in fairy tales... Perhaps ...intellectual shamans and others can serve as a peer group for evaluating different types of writing. It could be a subgroup of the Academy, even.

Another commented, "One [avenue to gauge external impact] is to give an award for these kinds of activities, perhaps for the best op-ed in Management".

vii   *Change Reward Structures:* As one scholar remarked, "the incentive systems are not aligned [to do impactful scholarship]. Until you get tenure, you produce in high-quality journals. There is no incentive to do impactful research. There is no incentive to do inter-disciplinary research even after tenure". Another reiterated: "Our evaluation systems are imperiling external impact and incentivizing the wrong behaviors". Others highlighted the influence of tenure and promotion criteria:

> People orient their work towards what gets tenure. So, in the field of Management, we tend not to research real-life problems, do not work enough with governments, and do not publish in vehicles that influence business policy and practice or government policy and practice...We do have vehicles that reach managers, but these do not count for much in the academic evaluation of an individual's research record...How do you make an impact if your promotion is based on 4* publications which are designed for other academics rather than business or government or NGOs?

Some argued for different weights placed at different stages of academic careers: "From Assistant to Associate, I would place 100 percent weight on writing articles for top-ranked journals. From Associate to Full Professor a greater proportion of the evaluation, perhaps 50 percent, should be paid to activities that may impact practice".

viii   *Provide Mentoring:* Some scholars argued for new role models in academics. As one stated, "Public advocacy is important. But our advice for new scholars is on how to play the journal-ranking game, not how to make a difference. This is a big mistake". Senior scholars could play a big role in increasing scholarly impact. Another scholar stated:

> Senior people, after getting tenure, should concentrate doing and mentoring the value-added of their work on policy and practice. Our senior professors should lead the way. Stop

obsessing with publishing in 4* journals. Senior professors should encourage junior faculty to publish books, write for practitioner-oriented journals, etc. But, people do not want to muddy the water.

Another scholar argued for different strengths that senior scholars may bring in other regions of the world.

The AOM should look at seniority in a different way in the U.S. and other countries. Senior European faculty may not be trained in American ways of publishing research, but they have good ideas. Also, these faculty have been trained in their own language, French, or whatever. They do not have the same research and writing style as in the U.S. Some local researchers are never translated into English. References and citations become an issue. We lose a lot.

In conclusion, this book constitutes a journey of exploration into the meanings and understandings of scholarly impact by members of a major academic association specifically, with results and recommendations generalizable to the social sciences. Distrust in established metrics to gauge quality and impact has eroded publics' and students' trust: perhaps over optimistically, *Times Higher Education* (2021) concluded that "universities are moving to a more holistic assessment of their research culture after an over-reliance on quantitative data led to narrow thinking and misrepresentation". Regardless, humanity faces what *The New York Times* columnist Thomas Friedman (2019) referred to as a "hugely plastic moment", including but not limited to anthropomorphic changes to physical environments, globalization of national and regional economies, rapid ascensions of artificial intelligence, and changes in communication technologies. Though mostly technological, these developments, occurring at unprecedented speeds, are contributing to disruptions of the world's economies, mass migrations, changes in social interactions, and political upheavals, with impacts that extend from individuals' daily experiences to the planet's ecosphere. The hard sciences are developing technological solutions to these challenges; but the processes that unleash these changes and mediate their consequences remain inherently social, unfolding on human scales, the domain of Management researchers. Management scholars uniquely possess the expertise, theoretical perspectives, and research tools to make sense of these developments, as well as, potentially, to propose policies to manage them.

The conversation so far appears sobering. Despite well-articulated measures of scholarly impact, widespread and deep concerns exist on their validity, reliability, and the benefits of our research to society. As one respondent commented in the survey, if we cannot have impact, "At least do no harm". Yet, some evidence exists that by focusing evaluations of impact almost entirely on outputs that generate little measurable value for society, and meager interest from external constituencies, we run the risks of doing harm through misallocating resources both locally and globally, marginalizing issues of concern to many, increasing cynicism, and thereby affecting lives and careers. Unlike the Roman Empire, calls for institutional change and reevaluations have increasingly come not from barbarians at the gate, but from prominent citizens. We hope you join the conversation.

References

Academy of Management Perspectives (2021). Learn more about *AMP*, 2021. https://journals.aom.org/journal/amp

Aguinis, H., Suárez-González, I., Lannelongue, G., & Joo, H. (2012). Scholarly impact revisited. *Academy of Management Perspectives, 26*(2), 105–132.

Friedman, T. (2019). Has our luck run out? *New York Times*, Opinion, April 30.

Grant, M., Vernall, L., & Hill, K. (2018). Can the research impact of broadcast programming be determined?. *Research for All, 2*(1), 122–130. doi:10.18546/RFA.02.1.11.

Hambrick, D. C. (1994). What if the academy actually mattered?. *Academy of Management Review, 19*(1), 11–16.

Kassab, O. (2019). Does public outreach impede research performance? Exploring the 'researcher's dilemma' in a sustainability research center. *Science and Public Policy, 46*(5), 710–720.

Piwowar, H., Priem, J., Larivière, V., Alperin, J. P., Matthias, L., Norlander, B., Farley, A., West, J., & Haustein, S. (2018). The state of OA: A large-scale analysis of the prevalence and impact of Open Access articles. *Peer J* 6:e4375. https://doi.org/10.7717/peerj.4375

Research Excellence Framework (REF) (2021) https://www.ref.ac.uk/

Times Higher Education (2021). Restoring trust in research metrics to repair student and public confidence. April 30. https://www.timeshighereducation.com/hub/clarivate/p/restoring-trust-research-metrics-repair-student-and-public-confidence?utm_source=Eloqua&utm_medium=email&utm_campaign=EM_1_May_Newsletter_Research_Smarter_SAR_Global_2021_Librarians_1B

Zardo, P., Barnett, A. G., Suzor, N., & Cahill, T. (2018). Does engagement predict research use? An analysis of The Conversation Annual Survey 2016. *PLoS ONE, 13*(2), e0192290. https://doi.org/10.1371/journal.pone.0192290

Appendix 1

Team members of the Academy of Management's Strategic Doing project

Team 1 – Meaning & Constituencies of Scholarly Impact – Name	Employer Affiliation (at beginning of project)
José Ernesto Amorós	ESADE Business School, Mexico
Neal Ashkanasy	University of Queensland, Australia
Frédérique Alexandre-Bailly	ESCP Europe Business School, France
David Boje	New Mexico State University
Marc Bonnet	University of Lyon, France
Cary Cooper	Manchester Business School, UK
Thomas Cummings	University of Southern California
Usha Haley	West Virginia University
Christine Quinn Trank	Vanderbilt University
Ian Mitroff	University of Southern California and University of California Berkeley
Carlos Osorio	Adolfo Ibanez School of Management, Chile
Tyrone Pitsis	Leeds University, UK
José Luis Rivas	ITAM Business School, Mexico
Karlene Roberts	University of California Berkeley
Howard Thomas	Singapore Management University, Singapore
Maria José Tonelli	Fundacao Getulio Vargas (FGV), Brazil
Anne Tsui	University of Notre Dame & Arizona State University
Kuo Frank Yu	City University Hong Kong, Hong Kong

(Continued)

Team 2 – Disseminating Knowledge to Non-Academics – Name	*Employer Affiliation (at beginning of project)*
Jyoti Bachani	St. Mary's College
Christof Backhaus	Newcastle University, UK
Melanie Cohen	U.S. Department of Housing and Urban Development
Chris Dembek	University of Melbourne, Australia
Kathryn Goldman Schuyler	Alliant International University
William Guth	New York University
Thomas Mierzwa	University of Maryland University College
Miguel Olivas-Lujan	Clarion University of Pennsylvania
Fedor Ovchinnikov	Center for Evolutionary Leadership
René Pellissier	University of the Western Cape and University of Pretoria, Africa
Isaias Ruiz	ITESM, San Luis Potosi, Mexico

Appendix 2

AOM survey on measuring scholarly impact

MEASURING SCHOLARLY IMPACT SURVEY ©
Academy of Management, 2017, all rights reserved.

This survey is part of an AOM Strategic Initiative. It cannot be copied, distributed, or used in part or whole without explicit permission from the Academy of Management.

Dear Academy Member,

Invitation to Participate in a Survey on the Changing Nature of Scholarly Impact
Greetings. We are writing with a request: Would you be willing to take a survey that will help the Academy of Management to understand the issues that members are facing regarding scholarly impact? We are seeking feedback from a group of randomly selected members, including you, as part of an Academy initiative in which we are evaluating how we can respond strategically to changes in the profession. Your participation is vital for ensuring that the results accurately represent the thoughts and opinions of our members around the world.
The survey deals with how scholarly impact is understood and valued by the Academy's direct and indirect

stakeholders. Our plan is to use the results of the survey to improve the Academy's resources for supporting research, teaching, and engagement with practice.

Please participate in the anonymous survey by clicking on the button below:
Measuring Scholarly Impact (AOM)
There are a total of 14 questions, and the survey should take less than ten minutes to complete. Please complete the survey in one sitting as partial responses will not be saved. You can only take this survey once. The survey will be active for four (4) weeks and will close at midnight (EST) on *Thursday, November 17, 2016.*
Please do not forward the survey link to anyone. Your answers are strictly confidential and anonymous. The Academy of Management reserves all rights to the survey and data, and a full report of the results will be made available to members.
For technical and general questions on the survey, please contact survey@aom.org. For substantive questions on the survey and its use, please contact Professor Usha Haley, Project Champion.
Thank you again for your valuable time and input!

Usha C. V. Haley, PhD
Project Champion, Measuring Scholarly Impact
Practice Theme Committee Co-Chair

This survey is part of an AOM Strategic Initiative. It cannot be copied, distributed, or used in part or whole without explicit permission from the Academy of Management.

Q1 Please identify your current primary job title and level. Please check as many as may apply:

❐   Assistant Professor (US equivalent)/Lecturer (UK equivalent)
❐   Associate Professor (US equivalent)/Senior Lecturer (UK equivalent)
❐   Full Professor (US equivalent)/Reader (UK equivalent)
❐   Chaired Full Professor (US equivalent)/Professor (UK equivalent)
❐   Professor Emeritus (any rank)
❐   Dean/Associate Dean
❐   Adjunct/Part-time/Visiting University Professor (any rank)

☐ Research Professor (limited or no teaching expectations)
☐ Practice/Teaching Professor (limited or no research expectations)
☐ Businessperson/Consultant
☐ Government Employee
☐ PhD/Graduate Student
☐ Postdoctoral Researcher
☐ Unemployed
☐ Other Academic Rank (please specify) _____

Q2 In which region of the world are you primarily based? Please choose one:

○ Africa
○ Asia
○ Central America
○ Eastern Europe
○ European Union and the UK
○ Middle East
○ North America
○ Oceania
○ South America
○ The Caribbean

Q3 Please rank each of the following audiences for academic research in terms of importance.

1 = Very Unimportant, 2 = Unimportant, 3 = Neither Important nor Unimportant, 4 = Important, 5 = Very Important.

_____ Top management and decision-makers in companies
_____ Middle management in companies
_____ Lower management and non-managerial employees in companies
_____ Other academics in Management
_____ Other academics in the Social Sciences
_____ Students
_____ Media
_____ Government/policymakers
_____ Industry associations
_____ Non-governmental organizations
_____ Labor organizations
_____ Society as a whole

Q4 What other audiences, if any, would you consider important for academic research? Please write your answer below.

For the questions below, "scholarly impact" refers to an auditable or recordable occasion of influence arising out of research.

Q5 In general, please evaluate each of the following indicators of scholarly impact in terms of importance.

1 = Very Unimportant, 2 = Unimportant, 3 = Neither Important nor Unimportant, 4 = Important, 5 = Very Important.

_____ Scholarly articles in top-tier journals
_____ Scholarly articles in lower-ranked or unranked journals
_____ Articles in practitioner-oriented/industry publications
_____ Media use/coverage of research expertise
_____ Scholarly citations to research (e.g., in Web of Science, Google Scholar)
_____ Search-engine mentions (e.g., on Google, Yahoo)
_____ Consulting for business or government
_____ Invited keynote talks
_____ Presentations at academic conferences
_____ Direct regulatory influence (e.g., testimonies, legislative citations, expert witness)
_____ Invited public speeches
_____ Executive teaching
_____ Corporate or government board memberships
_____ Appearance on course reading lists
_____ Academic journals' editorial board memberships
_____ Op-eds, documentaries, media publications (e.g., in newspapers, blogs)
_____ Scholarly books
_____ Practitioner-oriented books
_____ Textbooks
_____ Book chapters
_____ Competitive research grants (e.g., NSF)
_____ Article downloads (e.g., through SSRN, publisher websites)
_____ Awards and honors for research
_____ Altmetrics (e.g., Researchgate RG scores)

Q6 What other indicators of scholarly impact do you see as important? Please write your answer below.

Q7 In your opinion, how important is it for calculations of scholarly impact to include the extent to which a scholar's work has affected or changed business practices? Choose one:

O Not at all important
O Somewhat important
O Moderately important
O Strongly important
O Intensely important

Q8 In your opinion, how important is it for calculations of scholarly impact to include the extent to which a scholar's work has affected or changed government policy? Choose one:

O Not at all important
O Somewhat important
O Moderately important
O Strongly important
O Intensely important

Q9 In your opinion, does interdisciplinary research that combines or draws substantially on two or more disciplines or fields of study (including but not limited to economics, psychology, political science, or sociology) have greater scholarly impact than research that draws on only one discipline or field of study? Choose one response:

O Definitely not
O Probably not
O Might or might not
O Probably yes
O Definitely yes

Q10 In which of the following ways does the university/institute/organization for which you work support pursuing scholarly impact? Please rank each of the following:
1= Strongly Disagree, 2= Disagree, 3 = Neither Agree nor Disagree, 4 = Agree, 5 = Strongly Agree.

_____ Through strongly considering publications in top-tier journals in tenure/promotion/evaluation decisions
_____ By giving a monetary reward for publications in top-tier journals

_____ Through strongly considering publications in practitioner journals in tenure/promotion/evaluation decisions

_____ Through strongly considering consulting activities in tenure/promotion/evaluation decisions

_____ Through strongly considering media coverage/testimonies/outreach in promotion/tenure/evaluation decisions

_____ Through strongly considering the obtaining of research grants in promotion/tenure/evaluation decisions

_____ Through strongly considering scholarly citations to research in promotion/tenure/evaluation decisions

_____ Through strongly considering published books in tenure/promotion/evaluation decisions.

Q11 In your opinion, does your university/institute/organization support you in your pursuit of the activities you believe are important for scholarly impact? Choose one:

O Never
O Almost never
O Sometimes
O Almost every time
O Every time

Q12 In your opinion, do journal rankings or journal lists reflect scholarly impact (e.g., Impact Figures in Thomson Reuters' Journal Citation Reports or Financial Times 50)? Choose one response:

O Definitely not
O Probably not
O Might or might not
O Probably yes
O Definitely yes

Q13 In your opinion, how much influence has management research had? Please rank each of the following:
1= Not at all Influential, 2 = Slightly Influential, 3 = Somewhat Influential, 4 = Very Influential, 5 = Extremely Influential.

_____ Government policy

_____ Management policy and practice in large enterprises in my country

_____ Management policy and practice in small- and medium-sized enterprises in my country

_____ Labor-management relations in my country
_____ Management theorizing
_____ Future research practice
_____ Teaching
_____ My students' career decisions

Q14 What do you believe an ideal measure of scholarly impact should include? Please write your answer below.

Thank you for your time! For technical and general questions on the survey, please contact xxx. For substantive questions on the survey and its use, please contact Professor Usha Haley, Project Champion and Practice Theme Committee co-Chair, at xxx or voice xxx.

Appendix 3

Overview of scholarly impact survey results

Usha C. V. Haley

The Academy of Management's (AOM's) survey went through two reviews at the level of the Board of Governors and had a response rate of 19 percent (700 responses out of 3,750 surveys sent). This section covers demographics, audiences for research, scholarly indicators of impact, scholars' impact on practice, scholars' impact on government policy, impact of interdisciplinary research, institutional support for scholarly impact, perceived validity of journal rankings and journal lists, and the influence of Management research.

1   **Demographics:** The results show that respondents came from all 15 ranks in academia that we had identified, with the top five as:

- Assistant Professor (US)/Lecturer (UK) 21 percent
- Associate Professor (US)/Senior Lecturer (UK) 19 percent
- PhD/Graduate Student 19 percent
- Full Professor (US)/Reader (UK) 15 percent
- Chaired Full Professor (US)/Professor (UK) 10 percent
  The geographic breakdown of the sample spanned all 10 identi-
  fied regions with the top five as:
- North America 57 percent
- EU and UK 27 percent
- Asia 8 percent
- Oceania 4 percent
- South America 1 percent
  Because of the sparse number of respondents from some areas,
  for regional statistical analyses, we collapsed some of the data
  into regional groupings based on historical and geographic ties.
  Specifically: (1) Central America/South America/Caribbean –
  12 (1+10+1); (2) Africa/Middle East – 15 (3+12); (3) Eastern
  Europe/EU/UK – 193 (6+187); (4) Asia – 55; (5) Oceania – 29;
  (6) North America – 394

2 **Audiences for Research:** The average of the importance of 12 audiences for academic research on a five-point scale from Very Unimportant to Very Important, ranged from a low of 3.29 (lower management and non-managerial employees in companies) to a high of 4.48 (other academics in Management). The average of the top-five audiences for academic research were:

- Other academics in Management 4.48
- Top management and decision-makers in companies 4.26
- Government and policy-makers 4.08
- Other academics in the social sciences 4.06
- Students 4.0

3 **Scholarly Indicators of Impact:** The average of the importance of 24 indicators of scholarly impact on a five-point scale from Very Unimportant to Very Important ranged from a low of 3.26 (scholarly articles in lower-ranked or unranked journals) to a high of 4.49 (scholarly articles in top-tier journals). The average of the top-five indicators of scholarly impact were:

- Scholarly articles in top-tier journals 4.49
- Scholarly citations to research 4.21
- Scholarly books 3.94
- Competitive research grants 3.93
- Articles in practitioner-oriented/industry publications 3.88

4 **Scholars' Impact on Practice:** The AOM's membership identified the importance for calculations of scholarly impact to include the extent to which a scholar's work has affected or changed business practices. About 54 percent considered impact on practice as either strongly important (31 percent) or intensely important (23 percent); only 7 percent of the membership viewed impact on practice as not at all important as a component of scholarly impact.

5 **Scholars' Impact on Government Policy:** The AOM's membership identified the importance for calculations of scholarly impact to include the extent to which a scholar's work has affected or changed government policy. About 46 percent considered impact on government policy as either strongly important (27 percent) or intensely important (19 percent); only 10 percent of the membership viewed impact on government policy as not at all important as a component of scholarly impact.

6 **Impact of Interdisciplinary Research:** The AOM's membership identified if they viewed interdisciplinary research that combines or draws substantially on two or more disciplines or fields of study

(including but not limited to economics, psychology, political science, or sociology) as having greater scholarly impact than research that draws on only one discipline or field of study. About 59 percent viewed interdisciplinary research as probably more impactful (31 percent) or definitely more impactful (28 percent) than research that draws on one discipline; only 4 percent of the membership viewed interdisciplinary research as definitely not more important than research drawing on one discipline.

7 **Institutional Support for Scholarly Impact**: The AOM's membership identified the ways in which institutions support the pursuit of scholarly impact. Institutions were seen overwhelmingly as strongly considering publications in top-tier journals, with other activities receiving far less, if any, support. The average of the importance of eight indicators of institutional support on a five-point scale from Very Unimportant to Very Important ranged from a low of 2.32 (strongly considering consulting activities) to a high of 4.54 (strongly considering publications in top-tier journals). The average of the top-five indicators of institutional support for the pursuit of scholarly impact were:

- Strongly considering publications in top-tier journals 4.54
- Strongly considering scholarly citations to research 3.76
- Strongly considering the obtaining of research grants 3.64
- Strongly considering published books 3.07
- Strongly considering publications in practitioner journals 2.84

The AOM's membership also presented their views on whether the institutions at which they worked supported their own pursuit of activities that they personally believed had importance for scholarly impact. Most (47 percent) said sometimes. About 38 percent of the AOM's members said the institution supported their pursuit of activities for scholarly impact almost every time (27 percent) or every time (11 percent). About 16 percent of the AOM's membership indicated their institutions almost never supported (13 percent) or never supported (3 percent) their pursuit of activities that they believed were important for scholarly impact.

8 **Perceived Validity of Journal Rankings and Journal Lists:** The AOM's membership was asked if journal rankings or journal lists (e.g., Journal Impact Figures in Clarivate's Journal Citation Reports or Financial Times 50) reflected scholarly impact. The majority of the AOM's members (60 percent) indicated that rankings and lists probably did not (20 percent), definitely did not (8

percent), or might or might not (32 percent) reflect scholarly impact. A minority (about 41 percent) indicated that rankings and lists definitely reflected (7 percent) or probably reflected (34 percent) scholarly impact.

9 **Influence of Management Research:** The AOM's membership indicated how influential they thought Management research had been. Generally, the membership thought that Management research had been somewhat influential, but the greatest influence had been on other Management academics including what they currently research and will research and teach. The average of the importance of eight avenues for Management research's influence on a five-point scale from Very Unimportant to Very Important ranged from a low of 2.36 (labor-management relations) to a high of 3.91 (Management theorizing). The average of the top-five indicators of scholarly impact were:

- Management theorizing 3.91
- Teaching 3.63
- Future research practice 3.59
- Management policy and practice in large enterprises 2.84
- Students' career decisions 2.64

Index

Note: **Bold** page numbers refer to tables; *italic* page numbers refer to figures and page numbers followed by "n" denote endnotes.

Taylor & Francis Group
an **informa** business

Taylor & Francis eBooks

www.taylorfrancis.com

A single destination for eBooks from Taylor & Francis
with increased functionality and an improved user
experience to meet the needs of our customers.

90,000+ eBooks of award-winning academic content in
Humanities, Social Science, Science, Technology, Engineering,
and Medical written by a global network of editors and authors.

TAYLOR & FRANCIS EBOOKS OFFERS:

A streamlined
experience for
our library
customers

A single point
of discovery
for all of our
eBook content

Improved
search and
discovery of
content at both
book and
chapter level

REQUEST A FREE TRIAL
support@taylorfrancis.com

 Routledge
Taylor & Francis Group

 CRC Press
Taylor & Francis Group

Printed in the United States
by Baker & Taylor Publisher Services